Hazen G. Werner

Albert Schweitzer

The Man and His Work

JOHN DICKINSON REGESTER

THE ABINGDON PRESS
NEW YORK CINCINNATI CHICAGO

Printed in the United States of America

To
MOTHER

CONTENTS

FOREWORD

THE writer's personal interest in Dr. Albert Schweitzer, who had previously been known to him only casually as the author of *The Quest of the Historical Jesus,* dates from a period of study in Europe during the years 1923-24, when Schweitzer was securing there the financial means to restore his medical mission in Africa, the work having been interrupted by conditions incident to the World War. A reading of his *Philosophy of Civilization* was accompanied by contact with the impression made by his appearances in England, France, and Switzerland, and by conversation with men acquainted with him. This was followed by the opportunities for further knowledge of him provided by the publication of his books, *On the Edge of the Primeval Forest, Memoirs of Childhood and Youth,* and *Letters from Lambarene.*

As a person and as a thinker Doctor Schweitzer compels and holds attention.

Critics who attack philosophy because of its detachment from life are not unusual, but it is uncommon to find one like Schweitzer, in whom the criticism takes the form of a vital personal philosophy that has systematic relation to other spiritual fields, and that functions as a unifying and impelling factor in socially valuable activity. In his varied and vigorous expressions of life and thought he is one of the most interesting and dynamic figures of our time.

Since this introduction to the man and his work is designed for a general public, all Schweitzer's writings are referred to by English titles, even where there are no translations of the works. A list of English translations and of additional works is given at the end of the book. Where there are English translations they have been made the basis for quotations and references.

To The Macmillan Company I wish to express appreciation for their very generous permission to quote at considerable length from several books by Albert Schweitzer, of which they are the American publishers.

I am deeply indebted to Professor Edgar S. Brightman and Dean Albert C. Knudson, of Boston University, for counsel in the prosecution of a study of Schweitzer of which this book is to some extent an outcome. My wife has given constant advice and aid in the preparation and correction of manuscripts. My thanks are due, further, to Professors Georgia Reneau and Julius P. Jaeger, colleagues in the College of Puget Sound, for assistance in reading the manuscript. I make acknowledgment also to Professor Norman Kemp Smith, of Edinburgh University, who first stimulated my interest in Albert Schweitzer's *Philosophy of Civilization.*

JOHN DICKINSON REGESTER.

Tacoma, Washington.

ALBERT SCHWEITZER
THE MAN AND HIS WORK

Every age has people, servants, and conquerors; the only supreme good fortune of mankind is a great personality.—*Goethe.*

CHAPTER I

ALBERT SCHWEITZER

In the early years of this century a young Alsatian instructor in the University of Strassburg, Albert Schweitzer, produced a history of the critical study of the life of Jesus. It was a notable offering at a time when the proudest work of historical criticism was exhibited in this field, and was a practical service to all students of religion, the book being typical of the careful and thorough work of German scholarship. The famous theologian Professor Wernle wrote that there was no other survey of this investigation in any degree comparable with it.

But Schweitzer's *From Reimarus to Wrede: A History of the Investigation of Jesus' Life,* was not merely a record such as its title indicated. It introduced evaluation of the views which it surveyed and exhibited a unique conception of the life and thought of Jesus on the part of its author. In criticism of this phase of the book Professor Wernle remarked with some sharpness that its title should have been *From Reimarus to Schweitzer,* for he appeared to be the only survivor of the corpse-strewn field of critical combat.

The distinctive thing in Schweitzer's thought was his thoroughgoing application of eschatological interpretations. The current New Testament criticism attempted to dismiss many Messianic claims in the gospel records as additions to the text, and to treat the better authenticated passages as Jesus' expression of a new conception of Messiahship. Schweitzer, on the contrary, accepted as authentic the records that Jesus predicted the imminent end of the world and his early appearance in heavenly glory. This was not merely an incidental element in the teaching of Jesus, he further affirmed, but formed the heart of it, and these expectations governed the course of Jesus' life.

It had been for some time the project of liberal theologians, armed with the new historical and psychological methods, to reconstruct the figure of Jesus with historic reality. By spiritualizing his Messianic claims and rôle they had discovered a personality which seemed more real than the doctrinal

Redeemer of traditional theology. The picture appeared more reasonable, and therefore more true.

But to reconstruct the past by the rule of what is reasonable from our point of view is false historical procedure, Schweitzer protested. The real Jesus lived in the thought-life of his time, not of ours. The intellectual outlook to be attributed to him is not that in which we would feel most at home, but one which is alien and strange to us. It was not in his views about God's plans that he revealed God, but in his ethical spirit and in his self-immolation for humanity. These alone make an abiding and universal claim on men.

About Schweitzer's conception theological leaders agreed on scarcely more than its general unacceptability. That one of their clever young men had put forth the theory was understandable, a professor of the University of Strassburg explained in lectures at Oxford, because in the German universities the prevalence of these strange eschatological views would lead many of the recent students to regard them as the usual and normal ones.[1] Professor Jülicher, on the other hand, referred to it as a "startlingly original romance."[2] In England Professor Sanday at first welcomed the book, and acknowledged it as the basis of a full half of the lectures forming his *Life of Christ in Recent Research.*[3] But when this "splendid advertisement" was held responsible for getting it more appreciation than it had received in Germany,[4] Sanday forgot that he had said its conspicuous merit lay in the fact that from first to last the writer held a single clue firmly in his hand, and criticized its too consistent and logical use of the eschatological conception.[5]

Evidence for the theory in the thought and development of the early church was then presented by Schweitzer in a history of Pauline study. The verdict of theological leaders on his "consistent eschatology," however, was already given. Between its picture of Jesus and that which they had co-operatively been building there was not, Schweitzer himself had declared, any possibility of compromise. His work did not contribute to the development of their liberal interpretation of Jesus; and, as they proceeded with their program, it was disregarded. Occasionally in theological classes an idea of Albert Schweitzer's was mentioned in review of the possible interpretations of some difficult incident in the life of Jesus. A few preachers knew of his book as a work with which they should probably be acquainted, and others recognized him as author of certain ill-apprehended, but at any rate radical, views about Jesus. There were also musicians, commonly unaware of his relation to theology, to whom Schweitzer was known as Bach's biographer. Not many people, however, were acquainted with the man back of the theories and the books. Only a strange unorganized social group, members of a "fellowship of suffering," knew his spirit and character.

A few years after the close of the World War the general public in Europe began to hear of a Dr. Albert Schweitzer, who was trying to secure funds to continue a medical service which, with his own resources and the gifts of interested friends, he had been carrying on among the blacks of Equatorial Africa. Now he had published a series of philosophical lectures that had been delivered at Oxford; or, again, he had just given a brilliant organ recital in one of the capitals of Europe for the benefit of his mission. People began to identify him with the Albert Schweitzer they had previously heard of as a rationalistic higher critic. Some scholars turned back to his theological writings, and, in the light of his philosophical theories, secured a new impression of their meaning—or, in the light of his missionary activity, passed a different judgment on their spirit and influence. But now Schweitzer was first of all a personality, and only after that the theologian, the author, or the musician. The meaning of his thought was more apparent in his history than in his words. The scope of his genius, the breadth and warmth of his human sympathy, the vigor of his character were more unusual and impressive than the formulation of theories. "Humanity is well supplied with men who achieve notable results in the particular fields of human thought and in the professional groups," Oskar Kraus observed, "but it has been poor, and still is, in great prophetic, self-forgetful characters, in men of outstanding ethical purpose. Albert Schweitzer is that type of man."[6]

CHAPTER II

THE MAN[7]

ALBERT SCHWEITZER was born on January 14, 1875, in Upper Alsace. His father, an Evangelical minister, was, at the time, pastor in the town of Kaysersberg, but removed a few months later to Günsbach, which continued for the lifetime of the parents to be the family home. Here he passed what he called a delightful childhood, with the companionship of a younger brother and three sisters, one older than himself.

In the home were the influences of culture and of religion. In both the mother's and the father's line there was musical talent, joined in the former with clerical traditions and leanings and in the latter with schoolmasterly pursuits. Religious convictions were associated with the spirit of rationalism and tolerance. Rigid discipline was maintained, but with it respect was shown for the personalities and the convictions of the children. Though the mother was reserved about expressing affection, the relation between parents and children was one of confidence and companionship.

Ill health of the father and financial difficulties disturbed the joyousness of the home for some periods of Schweitzer's boyhood, and engendered constant anxiety and self-denial during much of his school life. Then a small inheritance from a distant relative banished the worst of the money worries, and during his university days, as he expresses it, "bright sunshine again lay upon my home."

His youth, he reports, was on the whole a happy one, in which the harmony and understanding between children and parents was one of the chief factors. The sense of exceptional and undeserved good fortune, and of responsibility for its privilege, constituted, Schweitzer relates, one of the two most profound experiences of his early years, the other being that of sympathy with the pain which exists in the world.

Schweitzer's formal education began in the village school. This was not customary for children from the professional classes of society, who commonly started directly in a preparatory school, but Schweitzer says he has all his life been glad for the experience. From it he derived a knowledge of the village children and a respect for their abilities and talents. In this experience are some of the roots of his social democracy and of his faith in the capacities of less fortunate social groups.

When nine years old he began attending the technical school at Münster. This was two miles from his home, and he walked back and forth each day. After a year, at the generous invitation of his godfather, who was director of the elementary schools of Mülhausen, he went to live with him and his wife, "Aunt" Sophie, in order to attend the preparatory school of that city. Life there was under strictest regulation, but was enriched by reading (for which he had a great passion), discussion, and music.

In formal class work Schweitzer was not at first a ready or receptive pupil. There was prophetic meaning, he considers, in the fact that when his father took him to school for the first time he cried all the way. He was too given to day-dreaming to be a good student; and in some things, such as interpretation of literature, he was not merely inattentive, he confesses, but even hostile, closing his mind to class discussions and following the guidance of his tastes. So poor were his reports for the first term at the Mülhausen Preparatory School that the principal arranged a conference with his father at which his withdrawal from school was considered. Then a new form-master won his admiration. The self-discipline of this instructor and his conscientious performance of even the smallest matter of class duty appealed to Schweitzer. Under this influence he became a good student and soon exhibited decided intellectual interests.

For languages and mathematics he had never any aptitude, but in history he showed marked ability. During his earlier school days this subject was his chief interest. The next was natural science, which he found "peculiarly stimulating."

A strong love for nature was from childhood a conspicuous element in Schweitzer's character. In the daily walks to school at Münster when he was nine he preferred to be alone in order that he might enjoy the beauties of nature in its seasonal changes.

He grieved over the decision to send him to Mülhausen "as if . . . being torn away from nature." This deprivation he felt keenly in the following years; and excursions which he was allowed to make when a few years older have a place among his cherished memories.

In nature he felt an absolute mysteriousness. The scientific textbooks and their confident explanations, "shaped and trimmed with a view to being learnt by heart . . . and . . . already somewhat out of date," did not satisfy him. Force, or Life, appeared to him as a forever inexplicable element. Here (and only to a slightly less degree in history) he was affected by a consciousness that knowledge was only more or less thorough description, while the process under investigation was full of riddles.

This sense of the problematic in nature and in human life led Schweitzer to philosophy. The study of the subject was begun at Mülhausen in the classes of the principal, Wilhelm Deecke, whose influence, Schweitzer thinks, was the most profound that affected him in these school days. "Forever memorable to me," he says, "are the hours in which he read Plato with us, and through that means introduced us to philosophy in general. . . . Only one who is acquainted with the profound moral spirit in which the instruction of this eminent and distinguished teacher was presented, can estimate the influence which he exercised upon his pupils."[8] Other forces also impelled him to philosophical reflection. As he entered theology, its connection with philosophy of religion in general gave this direction to his thought. Pressure for clarification in philosophical study came likewise from his æsthetic and artistic activities.

Schweitzer had a love for music from the earliest years of his life. He had found this love within the family circle, and to it attributes even hereditary force. Of his passion for the organ he says:

> It was born in me. My mother's father, Pastor Schillinger, of Mühlbach, had been deeply interested in organs and organ-building. He is said to have been a very fine improvisator. My father too possessed this gift. When a child I listened to him for hours together as he sat, in the dusk, at the old square piano, which he had inherited from Grandfather Schillinger, and gave rein to his imagination.[9]

Organ-playing never appeared to Schweitzer as a social accomplishment which had to be painfully acquired. Rather, it was a medium for thought and feeling, familiar from childhood, providing him his freest form of spiritual expression. To him, musical compositions were not things to be reproduced mechanically, but to be understood and re-expressed with personal independence.

Instruction, encouragement and opportunity to play were given him at an early age, both within the home and outside it. "Before I went to school," he says, "my father had already begun to teach me some music." In the church at Günsbach too, while he was still a child, he was permitted to use the organ, because of the organist's friendliness and in consideration of his usefulness as a substitute; and at the age of nine he was able to play for services.

Favorable circumstances were joined with a natural aptitude for music in Schweitzer. At the basis of this was a keen æsthetic sensibility. Some of his early experiences of music, he relates, stirred his emotions profoundly:

> When the vocal duet, "In the mill by the stream there I was sitting in quiet thought," was sung, followed by "Beautiful forest, who planted you there?" I had to hold on to the wall to prevent myself from falling. The charm of the two-part harmony of the songs overwhelmed me and flowed through my whole being. Similarly, the first time I heard brass instruments playing together I almost fainted from excess of pleasure.[10]

Several times in boyhood he attempted to represent in verse and drawing the impression made upon him by the beauty of nature. But this was without success. From then on, he says, "I devoted myself to the enjoyment of beauty simply through the eyes . . . and . . . never again tried either to draw it or to poetize about it. Only in musical improvisation have I . . . felt myself to have any creative ability."

The power of artistic expression was not lacking in Schweitzer, but music was its most ready channel. He early possessed facility in musical composition which he took as much for granted as the power of speech. An incident which illustrates this and which indicates also the sensitiveness and strength of his natural social sympathy is related in his memoirs:

It was my delight to improvise, and to reproduce songs and hymn-tunes with an accompaniment of my own invention. So now when in the singing lesson the teacher continually played the hymn-tune with one finger and no accompaniment, I found it far from pleasing, and during the interval I asked her why she did not play it properly with the harmony. Then in my enthusiasm I sat down at the harmonium and played it straight away to her out of my head, but with harmony in several parts. Then she became very friendly with me . . . but went on herself always picking out the tunes with one finger only. Then it occurred to me that I could do something which she could not, and I was ashamed of having made a show before her of my ability, which I had till then taken as something which I possessed as a matter of course.[11]

Serious study and discipline were demanded, however, for the sake of artistry. He recounts that while at the home of his godfather in Mülhausen: "After lunch I had to practice till it was time to go to school again," and in the evening "If I got my home-work finished early, I had to go to the piano again." That this discipline was not always willingly submitted to is indicated by reference to arguments with which his "aunt" hustled him to the instrument.

The music teacher, equally with his teachers in school, he says, "found at first little pleasure in teaching me." This was due in part to the fact that in the practice hours he played at sight and improvised instead of applying himself to the assigned piece, but even more to a reluctance to express his feelings in music before his teacher. His description of the incident which aroused him to genuine achievement is worthy of repetition at length:

I could not bring myself to display to him all that I felt while playing a beautiful piece of music, and I am sure that many music students feel the same. Thus it was that I irritated him with my "wooden playing." But one day when, still mastered by this prejudice, I had ground out a badly practiced sonata of Mozart's, he angrily opened a volume of Mendelssohn at the "Song Without Words" in E natural. "Really you don't deserve to have such beautiful music given you to play. You'll come and spoil this 'Song Without Words' for me, just like everything else. If a boy has no feeling, I certainly can't give him any!" "Oho," thought I to myself, "I'll show you whether I have any feeling or not!" And the whole week through I carefully practiced this piece, which I had so often played by myself. I even did what no one had ever got me to do yet—

I found out by experiment the best fingering, and wrote it above the notes. In the next lesson when the finger-exercises and scales were all finished, I braced myself up and played the "Song Without Words" just as my very soul bade me. My teacher said little, but putting his hands firmly on my shoulders, he moved me from the piano and himself played over to me a "Song Without Words" that was new to me. Next I was given a piece of Beethoven's, and a few lessons later I was found worthy to begin upon Bach. Then after a few more lessons it was disclosed to me that after my confirmation I should be allowed to have lessons on the big and beautiful organ in Saint Stephen's. Thus there came to fulfillment a dream long cherished in secret.[12]

Schweitzer was eighteen when his preparatory-school work was completed. He was ready and eager to go on to the University. Training in theology and preparation for the ministry were his objectives, after the usual arts course. With this program, he was resolved that the study of music was also to be continued.

An acquaintance with the distinguished French organist Charles Marie Widor was formed in the fall in which he entered the University. This was the beginning of a friendship and co-operation which developed in subsequent years. The older musician has written of the incidents:

In the autumn of 1893 a young Alsatian presented himself to me and asked if he could play something on the organ to me.

"Play what?" I asked.

"Bach, of course," was his reply.

In the following years he returned regularly for longer or shorter periods, in order to "habilitate" himself—as they used to say in Bach's day—in organ-playing under my guidance.

One day in 1899, when we were going through the chorale preludes, I confessed to him that a good deal in those compositions was enigmatic to me. "Bach's musical logic in the preludes and fugues," I said, "is quite simple and clear; but it becomes cloudy as soon as he takes up a chorale melody. Why these sometimes almost excessively abrupt antitheses of feeling? Why does he add contrapuntal motives to a melody that have often no relation to the mood of the melody? Why all these incomprehensible things in the plan and working out of these fantasias? The more I study them the less I understand them."

"Naturally," said my pupil, "many things in the chorales must seem obscure to you, for the reason that they are only explicable by the texts pertaining to them."

I showed him the movements that had puzzled me the most; he translated the poems into French for me from memory. The mysteries were all solved. During the next few afternoons we played through the whole of the chorale preludes. While Schweitzer—for he was the pupil—explained them to me one after the other, I made the acquaintance of a Bach of whose existence I had previously had only the dimmest suspicion. In a flash it became clear to me that the cantor of Saint Thomas' was much more than an incomparable contrapuntist to whom I had formerly looked up as one gazes up at a colossal statue, and that his work exhibits an unparalleled desire and capacity for expressing poetic ideas and for bringing word and tone into unity.[13]

Schweitzer's interest in music and his interest in religion were in most intimate relation. In times of religious feeling he was particularly conscious of the harmony of music with the thoughts of his heart, and undoubtedly at such times he was impelled by its moving power.

The music of Bach, to which Schweitzer's concern with music is practically limited, is profoundly religious. For him "music is an act of worship," Schweitzer says; "his artistic activity and his personality are both based on his piety." "Bach's real religion," he explains, "was not orthodox Lutheranism, but mysticism. In his innermost consciousness he belongs to the history of German mysticism." "What speaks through his works," C. M. Widor has also written, "is pure religious emotion, . . . the emotion of the infinite and the exalted. . . . His cantatas and Passions tune the soul to a state in which we can grasp the truth and oneness of things, and rise above everything that is paltry, everything that divides us."

Such were the influences which the music of Bach was exercising on the sensitive spirit of Schweitzer. The peculiar appeal of Bach to him throws light on the nature of his own most intimate religious experiences. A kinship of spirit is suggested in his attachment to the composer and in his sympathetic interpretation of him. Schweitzer himself confirms this when he says, "Only he who sinks himself in the emotional world of Bach, who lives and thinks with him, . . . is in a position to perform him properly."

Religious sensibility and piety are deeply planted in Schweitzer. His earliest recollections center about the church: the feel of the servant girl's cotton glove over his mouth when he yawned or sang too loud; the reflection of the organist in the organ-mirror, which disappeared when the preacher entered the pulpit, and which he thought was the devil; and the impression of quiet and solemnity. He says:

> From the services in which I joined as a child I have taken with me into life a feeling for what is solemn, and a need for quiet and self-recollection, without which I cannot realize the meaning of my life. I cannot, therefore, support the opinion of those who would not let children take part in grown-up people's services till they to some extent understand them. The important thing is not that they shall understand, but that they shall feel something of what is serious and solemn. The fact that the child sees his elders full of devotion, and has to feel something of their devotion himself—that is what gives the service its meaning for him.[14]

Influential also were the religious life of his home and additional religious instruction in school. Notable in the school teaching was that of Pastor Schäffler, a man of strong religious personality and more than average orator, who "could tell the Bible stories with entrancing effect."

In Schweitzer's religious life there has been throughout a strong element of personal feeling which approaches the mystical. The church of his youth was shared by Protestant and Catholic congregations, and a deep impression was made upon him by the seeming magnificence of the Catholic chancel flooded by sunlight, and by its windows through which "one looked out on a world which continued the chancel of the church into an infinity of distance, and was in turn flooded by a kind of transfiguring glory imparted to it by the chancel." In this manner, Schweitzer says, "my gaze wandered from the finite to the infinite, and my soul was wrapped in peace and quiet." For worship in general he feels that "the eye needs distance which lends itself to the mood of the worshiper, so that the outward gaze can change to the inner one."

This depth of religious feeling Schweitzer did not readily reveal. A natural reserve made him reluctant to manifest his sentiments even in friendliest personal relations. When he was preparing for confirmation at the age of fifteen, he could not bring himself to confess to the kindly inquiry of his pastor the thoughts with which he entered upon the step. The troubled clergyman spoke to his family of his apparent indifference; but "in reality," Schweitzer says, "the confirmation was a profound experience to me."

The serious pursuit of his training for the ministry did not suffer during the years in which Widor described him as periodically habilitating himself in organ-playing. In the spring of 1898 he took the state examination in theology, and won a scholarship which gave him opportunity for a year's study at other universities. One semester he spent at the Sorbonne and another at the University of Berlin. At their close he was granted the degree of Doctor of Philosophy, for which he presented a dissertation on *The Sketch of a Philosophy of Religion in the Critique of Pure Reason.* Later that year he published a larger work on Kant's philosophy of religion.

Back in Strassburg after the travel year, Schweitzer became assistant pastor in Saint Nicholas Church. To it he had long been attached by sentiment. During the Franco-Prussian War it had been served by a younger brother of his mother's who had given his life in ministering to his people.

Albert had been named for him; and the account of his self-forgetful deeds had been an oft-repeated story in childhood days.

Shortly after going to Saint Nicholas' Schweitzer published two books on the life of Jesus, dealing with the Last Supper and with the Messiahship and Passion. Appointment to the theological faculty of the University followed. This, however, did not terminate his connections with Saint Nicholas Church, which he continued to serve for ten years.

During this time there was brought to completion a work on Bach which Schweitzer had had in hand for several years. Widor had suggested that the same help which had been given him in the interpretation of Bach be made available to other French organists in written form. But to treat adequately the dramatic nature and meaning of this music required an account of the general place of dramatic music in the liturgy of the German churches of Bach's time, of biographical factors, and of the conditions of instrumentation at the period. The study had become a huge work when Schweitzer published it in 1904, and it took a place as the standard authority upon the great German musician. In recognition, the Paris Bach Society promptly made him its honorary organist.

Meantime a new purpose in life had been formed by Schweitzer, namely, to go as a medical missionary to the natives of Africa. Now thirty years old, a doctor of philosophy and doctor of theology, a minister and university instructor, author of several books and an internationally known musician, he began the study of medicine.

Other activities and works which Schweitzer had in hand were not dropped; they became the financial foundation of the new undertaking. The famous *From Reimarus to Wrede* (Eng. trans., *The Quest of the Historical Jesus*) made its appearance the year after the medical training was begun, and simultaneously a study of French and German organ-construction and playing. The medical course at the University of Strassburg was pursued, then special studies on tropical diseases at Paris. He had married,[15] and, in co-operation with his plan, his wife trained as a nurse.

The preparations, not only intellectual

but physical and financial, were extensive and long. In the years just before setting out to his chosen field, Schweitzer supplemented his theological writings by the history of the critical study of Paulinism and a work on the mental health of Jesus, gave organ recitals in many of the capitals of Europe, and in co-operation with Widor collected and edited the fugues and sonatas of Bach. At Easter time, 1913, eight years after the inception of the plan, he embarked for a French Evangelical mission station in Equatorial Africa, and set up a small hospital. To this he has since devoted his energies. The occasions for presentation of his *Philosophy of Civilization,* of lectures on Christianity in its relation to other world religions, of his memoirs of childhood, and of his story of the work in Africa have been during visits to Europe made necessary by war conditions and loss of health and financial support.

Almost boundless energy and activity, directed by a peculiarly sensitive sympathy with all human experience and a remarkably intense concern for the physical and spiritual fortunes of mankind, are the features which appear most prominently in Schweitzer's character. When confronted at any place by human misfortune, pain or difficulty, his helping response is spontaneous and unrestrained.

The practical activity and administrative work in which his sympathies involve him are not, however, direct expressions of his temperament. The vigor and ability with which they are carried on are representative; but he is more fundamentally and essentially a philosopher than an executive. The daydreaming of his youth belongs to his nature. He is first a thinker; though thought is not in him a substitute for action, but its initiator and guide. Schweitzer's biography is in reality the history of his ideas, the arrival at which for him involves eventual forthright expression and practical manifestation. His intellectual frankness and vigorous self-expression make their appearance only through victory over a native reserve. A protective reticence concealed his feelings in boyhood, but has yielded to the earnestness of his later intellectual life and the vigor of his convictions.

Upon those who meet him Schweitzer

makes a vivid impression. An English acquaintance gives this excellent word-picture:

> Imagine . . . a tall, handsome, powerfully built man . . . with an easy, natural manner . . . in the favorable acceptance of the term . . . a man of the world. An Alsatian by birth, and resident for long periods in Paris, he speaks French as readily as German; . . . he is an interesting talker, but beyond that he is one of those men whose personality tells directly. The impression which one receives from him, first, last, and all the time, is one of immense but well-disciplined energy. In any company he would count, and in any circumstances he would not be negligible.[16]

"He was the most impressive personality who came within my range." Thus wrote an American author and lecturer who had met Schweitzer and heard him speak to groups in Switzerland during the summer of 1927, after returning from "three months' travel, which in London and Geneva had given . . . sight and hearing of some of the most notable persons in the world."[17] "From whatever angle one may approach the man, Albert Schweitzer," says a German scholar, "one cannot fail to be captivated by the simple greatness and depth of his personality."[18]

The basis of such impressions is not merely the notable achievements of the man, but the directness and sincerity of his human fellowship, the sure appeal of his social reactions to sanctions in the general consciousness, and the vigor and enthusiasm of his convictions. Strength and gentleness, intellectual freedom and evangelical zeal are found combined in him. The effect is one not only of greatness but also of attractiveness.

These qualities of Schweitzer's character appear clearly in all the fields of his activity, and give them their coherence. As a musician, as a theologian, as a missionary, and as a philosopher there is a unity to his expressions which is the unity of his vigorous personality.

CHAPTER III

THE MUSICIAN

As a musician Schweitzer's name, as has been observed, is intimately linked with that of the great German composer and organist Johann Sebastian Bach. This is due primarily to the unsurpassed exposition of the musician which he has given in his thorough and interesting two-volume work, *J. S. Bach.* Four editions of the work have appeared in French, the same number in German, and two printings in English. Through rendition also he has been an interpreter of Bach's music, and has secured new understanding and appreciation of the difficult and long misunderstood old master. To his zeal, further, are to be credited extensive editions of Bach's compositions. Even in the isolation and activity of his African mission this labor was continued. An organ, inclosed in a metal case to protect it from white ants, went with him into the tropical wilds as a gift of the Paris Bach Society; and at noon siesta time, or in the evenings, he worked to prepare some of Bach's unknown pieces for publication.

To original composition Schweitzer has never actively applied himself. Music has never been his vocation, but has stood alongside the business of life as belonging to its spiritual expression and refreshment. For those purposes the music of Bach has provided a voice for his experiences and feelings.

Schweitzer's musical education is none the less broad and thorough. It is, in effect, that of a professional, involving not only technical facility, but also intimate acquaintance with the means of tone production, the history of music, the structure of musical instruments, the principles of musical composition, and the products of the musical art (so far at least as German music is concerned) with amazing fineness of detail. He performs with considerable ability on several musical instruments, but the organ is the one on which he is most accomplished and for which he has the greatest love. He is a critic of its construction as well as an artist in its playing, and has written with authority on French and German organ-building and playing.

Knowledge of the instrumental means of

tone production, even of the principles of music and laws of harmony and skill in execution, are to Schweitzer, however, merely subordinate matters. They relate, he considers, only to an essential apprenticeship on materials through which the spirit may speak. That which really makes an artist, he holds, is not a facility with tones, or paint, or tools, even though he would be mute without this, but an idea which dominates him and to which he gives expression according to the measure of his mastery of some medium which best suits him. The art-product is merely the language of a conception, a symbol which mediates between the æsthetic feeling of the producer and that of the listener or onlooker. That which constitutes the greatness of a work of art is not its formal perfection, but the worth of the spiritual conception which it embodies.

Musical compositions cannot be produced, Schweitzer points out, by mechanical operation of the laws of harmony, but must be expressions of the human spirit. The relation between the laws of harmony and musical composition is the same as that between the laws of good manners and men's social conduct. Just as the latter laws may sometimes be disregarded at the dictate of the heart, so the former may on occasion be overwhelmed by the vital flow of music, "which is superior to all laws."[19]

This assertion of the freedom of the spirit in relation to canons does not mean for Schweitzer a cult of beauty independent of other values. Here, as at every point, Schweitzer has before his eyes the contribution to human welfare, as in his securing a considerable part of the funds for his mission in Africa by giving Bach recitals in many of the capitals and leading cities of Europe. Of the "aunt" who in his boyhood admonished him, "You don't know what good your music mayn't be to you when you're grown up," he remarks that "Indeed, she could not have dreamed that one day my music would help me to collect the funds for starting a hospital in the primeval forest." Again in the years 1917-1923, which he spent in Europe regaining health and financial support for his work, he appeared in recitals in Paris, London, and other cities, manifesting an artistry which was acclaimed by the critics and which was eloquent alike of his zeal for human life and of his attachment to music during the strenuous years of medical work. Schweitzer thinks simply, and without apology, of a service of music to humanity. This, as a fact requiring no justification, is his first consideration. In his youth music provided æsthetic pleasure, emotional expression, and creative activity. In the furtherance of his work of mercy it was capable of giving help, in the cultural isolation of the tropics it could furnish inspiration, and in weariness from ministering to the sick it could refresh and encourage. For the religious attitude and ethical interest which are central in his philosophy, it is able to furnish another (the artistic) expression. A recital of Schweitzer's, the musical critic of a leading English newspaper wrote, was "not merely a display of brilliant technique, but an act of worship and a sacrament." His primary aim in the book on Bach was not to make a contribution to musical knowledge or to the correct execution of Bach's music, but to further the general performance of it in the hope that it would "help our age to attain the spiritual unity and fervor of which it so sorely stands in need."[20]

CHAPTER IV

THE THEOLOGIAN

Religion has always been an important element in life for Schweitzer and an object of immediate interest. Its relation to morality has further centered his activity upon it.

In all his studies, regardless of the immediate topic, the final question for Schweitzer is how our ethical ideals and conduct can be given a sound and permanent basis. His training and disposition insure that the religious foundations secure first consideration; and, on the other hand, his moral seriousness makes the ethical interest determinative in his theological studies.

The rational foundations for religion and morality offered by Critical Idealism were what Schweitzer sought in his early study of Kant's philosophy of religion. This work was not intended, he asserted in the preface, to be a criticism of Kant's philosophy of religion, but only a critical analysis of the various ideas of Kant which belong to the philosophy of religion. Notwithstanding these modest pretensions, the result was new light for the understanding and evaluation of Kant's thought on the objects of religious faith—self, God, and immortality.

Kant's philosophy of religion is commonly derived from the *Critique of Practical Reason* alone. By assembling the different treatments of the problems and comparing them, Schweitzer showed the development of Kant's thought, and brought his writings into a criticism of each other which reveals how far Kant actually realized his aims in reference to religious belief.

First in a brief sketch of a philosophy of religion presented in the *Critique of Pure Reason* (the three sections of "The Canon of Pure Reason"), and then in the *Critique of Practical Reason,* Kant had suggested that the ideas which Critical Idealism excluded from theoretical proof—immortality, freedom and God—could be established by reason in its practical activity. Schweitzer discovers, however, that the resultant linking of Kant's theoretical philosophy with morality is only apparent and not real.

The idea of freedom inevitably took the

primary position when Kant attempted a transition of the system of transcendental ideas to the realm of practical interest. But whereas the problem left unsettled by theoretical reason was the general question of natural causation, the freedom which is established in "The Canon of Pure Reason" is a practical one that lies within the realm of natural causation. It is a freedom that is limited to human action, and that is said to be demonstrable through experience.

In the *Critique of Practical Reason* Kant preserved a unity with his theoretical philosophy and actually dealt with the question of freedom in the natural order. This he was able to affirm, from the standpoint of Critical Idealism, by referring causality away from the natural, or "phenomenal," order to an order of transcendent reality. But in this case it is only theoretical, and not moral, interests that are satisfied. Since the natural order and the intelligible are not two different systems of reality, the moral order ceases to be something other than the natural, and the validity of moral distinctions and of moral judgments is denied. Kant, holding to the unestablished identity of the theoretical and practical ideas of freedom, regarded the original plan as carried out, but sensed the loss of moral significance to the extent of leaving freedom as the only idea of theoretical reason for which the plan of verification by reason in its practical use is consistently and completely carried out, and of claiming for the remaining ideas—God and immortality—only the status of postulates of the moral law.

That the moral question of freedom was not solved was evidenced by appearance of the problem how perfection, or change from evil to good, which is demanded by the moral law, is possible as free self-determination in the intelligible order. This shift in the question, from the natural necessity of action to its order, carries over the problem of freedom into the intelligible world itself, where it cannot again be solved by the device of distinguishing phenomenal and real agency.

Kant's suggestion of immortality as satisfaction of this moral demand for perfection does not solve the problem satisfactorily. It involves the very identification of metaphysical causation with moral action which was pointed out above and which makes moral discrimination meaningless. Further, it is only with difficulty that the idea of God is secured from this point of view, and then in no more intimate relation to morality than as guarantor of happiness to those who practice it.

This problem of moral freedom appeared only briefly in the *Critique of Practical Reason,* under the influence of strong ethical interest, since the problems and presuppositions of Critical Idealism governed that work. In the *Religion Within the Bounds of Pure Reason,* where it arose again, Kant met the ethical demand for perfection differently, by the notion of a judgment of moral worth in the timeless intelligence of God. It is a fact that the idea of God as moral judge came from historical Christianity, however, not from pure reason; and Critical Idealism nowhere arrived at an idea of God which related him in an integral way to morality.

The one line of thought along which alone Kant reached an ethical theism, in Schweitzer's view, appears in the third part of the *Religion Within the Bounds of Pure Rea-*

son. There he abandoned the individualistic point of view which had been dictated by Critical Idealism through its absorption in the conditions of individual knowledge, and which had been making the difficulty for the moral demand. The possibility of perfection he then based upon a moral community of mankind, whose realization stands as a moral duty of man. In relation to this duty, whose end is not in our finite power, he arrived at the concept of God. This line of thought, however, derives from an innate moral law, and is not only wholly independent of Critical Idealism, but has even nothing in common with it.

The idea of a perfected moral society appears in Kant again in the part of the *Critique of Judgment* which deals with judgments of purpose. There he spoke of it as a goal which, while it lay beyond nature, could be regarded as its end. In this way he secured the idea of God in intimate relation to morality and also to the natural world (as its source and ruler) without identifying the natural order with the moral and so destroying the validity of ethical purpose.

But the assumption of a relation to Critical Idealism stultified this course of thought in the *Critique of Judgment.* The idea of the perfected ethical community, in relation to which man was regarded as the goal of creation, was crowded out by the individualistic point of view, reference to immortality, and the concept of happiness which belonged to that system.

The significance of the third Critique, for Schweitzer, is chiefly in its preparation for the thought expressed in *Religion Within the Bounds of Pure Reason.* This last work is, in his judgment, by virtue of its social outlook and vitality, the high point of Kantian philosophy of religion. Its merits, however, depend directly upon the fact that it breaks its bond of relation to Critical Idealism.

That Kant failed to develop an ethical theism on the presuppositions of or within the limits of Critical Idealism was Schweitzer's conclusion. "A philosophy of religion governed by the presuppositions of Critical Idealism and oriented with reference to them is an incompatible compound," he says, and "the fully developed philosophy of religion of Critical Idealism dissolves itself."

Thus it was only through the ethical earnestness of Kant, overstepping the bounds of Critical Idealism, that a philosophy of religion was associated with the system.

The writings of Kant which deal with philosophy of religion, Schweitzer sums up, show a development in religious thought which is marked by increased ethical power and a decreased influence of the system of Critical Idealism. The positive elements of Kant's philosophy of religion have their source in an innate moral law, and they appear in the places where Kant unwittingly goes outside the limits of Criticism, impelled by the strength of his own ethical spirit.

In the early study of Kant's philosophy of religion there are already sketched in this way the lines of Schweitzer's mature ethical philosophy. It involves an element of skepticism which goes far beyond that of Kant, but which, in doing so, overthrows itself and finds a ground for belief and for dynamic moral life. To the fuller treatment of this philosophy we shall return later. Now we must take account of the writings which deal with Jesus and early Christianity. In them, after the manner of a musical composition, the same theme is repeated, but greatly enriched and deepened.

After the largely negative outcome of his search for a basis for our ethical ideals and activity in philosophy, the almost inevitable place for Schweitzer to look for their authority was to the field of historical religion. The attempt of modern theology to find in Jesus the source and foundation of our present ethical views is examined in his *Quest of the Historical Jesus.* What develops from the study is an epic-tragedy of a heroic search to find in history the ethical Teacher and Social Redeemer of modern Christianity, in the prosecution of which the inquiry destroyed its own inherent view. Summarizing this episode of rational theology, Schweitzer says:

It set out in quest of the historical Jesus, believing that when it had found him it could bring him straight into our time as a Teacher and Saviour. It loosed the bands by which he had been riveted for centuries to the stony rocks of ecclesiastical doctrine, and rejoiced to see life and movement coming into the figure once more, and the historical Jesus advancing, as it seemed, to meet it. But he does not stay; he passes by our time and returns to his own. What surprised and dismayed the theology of the last forty years was that, despite all forced and arbitrary interpretations, it could not keep him in our time, but had to let him go.[21]

The life of Jesus, as Schweitzer represents it, differs from that with which we are familiar, both as regards inner consciousness and outer circumstance. The public ministry lasted less than a year. After contact with John the Baptist, Jesus appeared in Galilee proclaiming the near approach of the kingdom of God. He expected this about harvest time, and so, after a few weeks at the most, he sent out his disciples to make known as speedily as possible what was to happen. He told them in plain words (Matt. 10. 23) that he did not expect to see them again in the existing age, but that the Parousia of the Son of man, identical with the dawn of the Kingdom, would take place before they could make a hasty journey through Israel to announce it.

Though thus publicly announced, the coming of the Kingdom was in a sense a secret. There was nothing in the outward circumstances to justify this prediction, or that of imminent suffering such as was foretold at the sending out of the Twelve. The grounds were not historical, but were in the subjective ethical earnestness of Jesus cast in the doctrinal mode of the time.

Jesus had also a second secret—the conviction that in the "time of the end" he was destined to be the Messiah. The only persons to whom this was revealed were Peter, James, and John, until Peter, in spite of a promise of secrecy, inadvertently let it be known to the other disciples. About it Jesus enjoined secrecy upon the Twelve, but Judas revealed it to the high priest, and its confession by Jesus, under question, was the ground of his condemnation.

A third secret, that of the Passion, developed after the return of the Twelve from their mission, and on account of the delay of the Kingdom and of its antecedent period of suffering. Jesus' conviction of the imminence of these events was not weakened, but, since they did not come, it seemed that something, beyond the movement of repentance, had to be done. Jesus conceived that God had heard the prayer for deliverance from tribulation which had accompanied that for the coming of the Kingdom, and had made possible its vicarious accomplishment in a definite voluntary suffering in his own person. He accordingly went up to Jerusalem with the purpose of suffering for others and thus bringing in the divine Kingdom.

In this representation of the life of Jesus there are several especially striking and significant differences from the usual picture. Jesus' kingdom of God was a wholly future one, and was to be established by divine intervention.[22] Of it Jesus was not a founder, but merely an announcer. His difference from John the Baptist was only in his secret Messianic consciousness. Not only was his Messiahship not proclaimed to the public, or suspected by it, but it was for Jesus himself a wholly future state in which he was to appear in the universal transformation.[23] In no case did Jesus use the term "Son of man," as theologians have supposed, for an existent, humble, ethical Messiahship, or to educate the public to such a conception. He had two uses of the term, one with those who knew his secret, and another with the uninitiated, in which it was not apparent that he thought of himself as identical with the coming Son of man.[24] Jesus' purpose in general was not pedagogic. He sought to educate neither the public nor his disciples. The prediction of the coming of the Kingdom was his only message; beyond that his words were in parables containing a supernatural knowledge which was only for those who had ears to hear—that is, who were chosen of God. That his ministry was not one of teaching was determined by the fact of his apocalyptic outlook. This involved also the further consequence that Jesus taught no positive ethics, but only a probationary righteousness in view of the impending "end of all things."[25] Social situations and ethical precepts would be transcended in the Kingdom upon whose threshold they stood, and what Jesus taught was "a transition-ethics." It was not meant to be a permanent and universal code of conduct, but a statement of what was fitting as occasion and as preparation for the coming of the Kingdom. It was not an absolute ethics, but relative.

With the death of Jesus, however, the divine intervention in human affairs did not occur. There was no apocalyptic coming of the Kingdom nor Parousia of the "Son of man." The early Christian Church accordingly began to reconstruct both its eschatology and its Christology. Jesus, who had not thought of himself as a present but only as a future "Son of man," was represented as Messiah in his earthly life. This reconstruction of viewpoint occurred in some measure even in Mark, but appeared most fully in the Gospel of John. The latter deliberately transformed the eschatological elements, and destroyed the historical Jesus in order to present his earthly life as that of the Messiah.[26] There arose the conception of a spiritual Messiahship and of an inner Kingdom. The "transition-ethics" became an absolute ethics. The eschatological expectations were transformed into the Christian conception of immortality.

In advancing such a new and divergent conception of the ministry of Jesus, Schweitzer put himself under obligation to show how this set of beliefs and events developed into early Christian theology. If there is no natural and possible transition, the theory is condemned by the facts of history, regardless of its success in dealing with the gospel material. Schweitzer recognized this responsibility, and undertook the further inquiry in a historical review of the critical study of Paul. The work follows the general method of that which dealt with the critical study of Jesus; but instead of attaching his own views to the historical survey, Schweitzer reserved them for a later work.

The problem of Pauline study, according to Schweitzer, "consists in the two great questions: what Paul's doctrine has in common with primitive Christianity, and what it has in common with Greek ideas." For the critical investigations which he surveys he has no such praise as he bestowed upon the studies of the life of Jesus. Due to want of plan, the inquiry "has nothing very brilliant to show for itself in the way of scientific achievement," he says, despite the lavish expenditure of learning upon it. The history of the Pauline study, nevertheless, gives decisive answer, he declares, to the second of the fundamental questions above. The answer, as Schweitzer states it, is that "Paulinism and Hellenism have in common their religious terminology, but, in respect of ideas, nothing. The apostle did not Hellenize Christianity. His conceptions are equally distinct from those of Greek philosophy and from those of the Mystery-religions."[27]

For the demonstration of this position two general types of considerations are offered. The first is that when the assumption of Hellenic influence has been adhered to with courage and logical consistency, it has led to results which are compatible only with a radically altered tradition and history of Christianity, in which either the oldest Christian writings are referred to the second century or else Christianity is regarded as originally a product of Hellenistic-Oriental syncretism. On the other hand, Schweitzer says, "An explanation which shows that the apostle's system is based on the most primitive eschatological premises, and at the same time makes it intelligible why subsequent generations could not continue to follow the road on which he started, thereby demonstrates his primitive Christianity and, to this extent, also the genuineness of his chief Epistles."[28]

The second objection which Schweitzer urges against finding Hellenic influences in Paul is that the alleged affinities cannot stand an examination which takes account of their real essence and of differences in which the analogous features are conditioned. Paul's doctrines of sacraments and of redemption are the features which are sometimes referred to the Mystery-religions, since they are without analogy in Late Judaism. After cautions that Paulinism must be distinguished from any general New Testament religion governed by Johannine doctrine, and that the full development of Mystery-religions was reached only after Paul's time and then in no such definite form as those who assert this influence assume, Schweitzer considers these in detail. So far as the cultus meal is concerned, he says, all that is certain is that in both cases such a meal existed, while no connection, direct or indirect, has been shown; and it would be only by violence to his words that anyone could ascribe to Paul the conception of a sacramental eating and drinking of the body and blood of Christ. The attachment of significance to lustrations belongs to all religions, and does not constitute a connecting peculiarity. For Paul's distinctive conception of baptism, which has nothing to do with purification but effects a possession of pneuma, the Mystery-religions have no analogy.[29]

Of the fact that Paul does not present a Hellenization of Christian thought, his relation to the later history of dogma would give further evidence, Schweitzer says. It is in the doctrine of rebirth, as has already been noted, that Paul differs from both John and the Mystery-religions. The differences which exist between Paul and Jesus are also differences between the early Christian community and Jesus, which arose as the logical consequences of his death and resurrection. The most radical change in Christian thought (due to the delay in fulfillment of the expectation) was the decline of the eschatological element, and it falls between Paul and the fourth Evangelist. The fact is, that Christian dogma does not, and through the force of historical development could not, base itself upon Paul. It is through recognition of the eschatological character of his doctrines that the fact of its independence from him becomes understandable.

Though Schweitzer does not profess to

make a constructive investigation of Pauline doctrine in *Paul and His Interpreters,* it is apparent that he goes considerably beyond a historical survey. Not only does he criticize the attempts to find elements of Greek philosophy and Oriental Mystery-religions in Paul, but he makes the positive suggestions that all that is distinctive in the mission and doctrine of the apostle to the Gentiles, including his universalism and his attitude toward the Law, develops naturally out of Late Judaism and of the Christian intensification of the eschatological expectations, and that the apparent confusion and lack of unity in Pauline doctrine may be resolved in the eschatological viewpoint. It makes fewer contributions of philosophical ideas than does *The Quest of the Historical Jesus,* but the tendencies of the author flash out in the concluding paragraph, where he says:

> It may no doubt prove to be the case that this "positive" criticism will appear distressingly negative to those who look for results which can be immediately coined into dogmatic and homiletic currency.
>
> Their opinion, however, is of small importance. It is the fate of the "little-faiths" of truth that they, true followers of Peter, whether they be of

the Roman or the Protestant observance, cry out and sink in the sea of ideas, where the followers of Paul, believing in the Spirit, walk secure and undismayed.[30]

Some further definition of Schweitzer's attitude toward eschatology is required. In regarding the thought of Jesus and of the early church as dominated by eschatological expectations, Schweitzer does not, as some have supposed, mean to force these upon Christianity as essential to it. He considers that although Jesus, in accepting them, related himself in a normal and earnest way to the most spiritual and ethical element in the religious life of his time, to cherish such a hope to-day, after the course of history has shown that it is not God's plan, is fantastic. While Jesus' outlook was other-worldly and world-negating, our modern view must be world-accepting, in conscious opposition to that of Jesus, Schweitzer says. When we are freed from dogmatic supernatural prepossessions such as ruled in the thought-world of Jesus, world-affirmation, in fact, occurs in us automatically; but if it is to be Christian, it must be a spiritual affirmation in tension with world-negation such as appears in the sayings of Jesus. The optimistic and affirmative spirit must not be one of acceptance of the world, but is to stand in contrast to it, even though its end is not transcendental and its spirituality is related to earthly existence. Genuine religion and morality must derive from the personal spirit, not from the world.

Men feared that to admit the claims of eschatology would abolish the significance of Jesus' words for our time, Schweitzer says:

> But in reality that which is eternal in the words of Jesus is due to the very fact that they are based on an eschatological world-view, and contain the expression of a need for which the contemporary world with its historical and social circumstances no longer had any existence. They are appropriate, therefore, to any world, for in every world they raise the man who dares to meet their challenge, and does not turn and twist them into meaninglessness, above his world and his time, making him inwardly free. . . .[31]

Thus, though the particular world-view of Jesus was transient, the spirit of his life was eternal. What is to be sought from him is not a model for one's own life or thought, but the impression of his words, which, independent of historical knowledge, are able to convey their meaning and to work their effect in the life of the individual, if only modern theology does not for the sake of peace deny the world-negation in them.

It should be already apparent that in interpreting Jesus' outlook as eschatological, Schweitzer does not think of depreciating either his significance or his person. It is his assumption throughout all his discussion that Jesus was not a visionary enthusiast in devoting himself to the actualization of the eschatological expectations, but a morally earnest spirit addressing himself to the most vital feature in his spiritual inheritance. He attempts, however, in a dissertation which he presented at the University of Strassburg for the degree of Doctor of Medicine, and which he later published in slightly enlarged form,[32] to give a thorough examination to Strauss' oft-repeated suggestion that Jesus was somewhat psychopathic. Along with the special obligation for this investigation which he acknowledges as a result of his conclusions in the historical field, he points, quite properly, to his unique qualifications for the task as established by his former theological and historical studies and his medical training.

Schweitzer first makes the criticism of the writers who have interpreted Jesus' consciousness as pathological, that they are uncritical in their choice and use of sources. In a sketch of the results of critical study of the literature, Schweitzer excludes the Talmud and Apocryphal Gospels and the single tradition of Luke, and urges caution about the fourth Gospel, from whose doctrinal representation of Jesus three fourths of the evidence of mental abnormality is drawn. Matthew, with the exception of the first two chapters, and Mark, allowing for some misunderstandings and confusion of the tradition, are regarded as dependable, and in certain particulars as of striking genuineness.

Schweitzer sketches the life of Jesus briefly and on the lines of his earlier writings. Of the period before Jesus' public ministry little is known. With four brothers and some sisters, he was a member of the family of a carpenter. That he was descended on his father's side from David, Schweitzer thinks, "can be accepted as true," though this claim has been represented as an instance of the expansive disposition of paranoia. The public ministry was characterized throughout by the proclamation of the nearness of the kingdom of God. The implications of this message did not need to be described in detail, for the system of thought was familiar to the hearers. Of the ruler of the future Kingdom, however, there were diverse conceptions. The prophetic expectation of a descendant of David, and the apocalyptic notion of a heavenly being who would have the form of a "Son of man," were both current. For this unreconciled contradiction, Jesus, in the expectation of the imminent appearance of the Kingdom, had a personal solution, namely, that he was appointed to the dignity of future Messiahship, and that in the transformation to be effected by the coming of the Kingdom he would be revealed as "Son of man." This he did not include in his proclamation of the Kingdom, and only toward the last did it become known to his disciples. By its betrayal it became the occasion of his death, which he welcomed as the vicarious fulfillment of the sufferings of the final time through which he might usher in the Kingdom.

No matter how strange these ways of thinking may be to us, the conceptions which Jesus took over from tradition and held in common with his contemporaries cannot be regarded as pathological. His unique conception of the Messiah as one born an earthly descendant of David and exalted in the universal transformation at the dawn of the new age to the supernatural status of Messianic "Son of man" was the only natural reconciliation of the Davidic and Apocalyptic expectations which were current. Taken with the belief in the imminence of the events, prepared for by John the Baptist, it meant that the future Messiah was already to be found among the living descendants of David and was destined as a human being to endure with men the preparatory period of suffering, or, as Jesus came to think, to undergo it in their behalf. That Jesus' mental outlook was the mark of a psychopathic condition, Schweitzer says, is a judgment that "cannot endure the criticism of either the critical historian or the psychiatrist."[33]

The historic Jesus, according to Schweitzer, belongs to his own age and will not be modernized. Historical study, when it is sincere, and has given up its apologetic purpose, destroys the modern picture which it has made; and the figure which appears is one that to us, in our different thought-system, is enigmatic and strange.

Schweitzer's historic Jesus, it becomes evident, is not one to whom the religion of the present can ascribe its own thoughts and ideas. He will not serve as the authority for its humanitarian ideals. So far as this hope is concerned, Schweitzer concludes "there is nothing more negative than the result of the critical study of the life of Jesus."[34] Not only are our religious and ethical ideas not developed from critical philosophy, but they are not secured from Jesus nor certified by him.

But that hope, after all, Schweitzer decides, was a false one. The merit of the historical study is that it has destroyed it. The determination to find its world-accepting ethic in Jesus was the chief weakness of modern theology. To seek the content and authority of its outlook and ideals in history, where they did not exist, falsified history and hobbled the free dynamic expression of its own spirit.

The mood of world-affirmation which belongs to us, and which we cannot give up, is not to be found in Jesus. But it is not the outlook within which the spirit of Jesus was manifested that is of value, but the spirit itself; it is not his theoretical view that is significant, but the spirit in which, within the framework of his eschatological conception, he set himself to the task of occasioning the divine establishment of the Kingdom and sought to fulfill in himself the suffering necessary to usher it in. Not in a historical reconstruction of the mind of Jesus, but in the experience of this spirit, which will combine with our positive attitude to the world, can an understanding of him be reached.

The outcome of the historical inquiry is emancipation from the dominance of the historical Jesus and relation to his living ethical spirit. This spirit is that which strives with irrepressible power toward the spiritualization of the present, though in a mood of world-affirmation which is in disagreement with the eschatological viewpoint of Jesus. It is as a stranger that Jesus comes to us, just as to the young men whom he called to be his disciples, Schweitzer declares, giving the same command to follow him; "and to those who obey him," he says, "whether they be wise or simple, he will reveal himself in the toils, the conflicts, the suffering which they shall pass through in his fellowship, and as an ineffable mystery, they shall learn in their own experience who he is."[35]

From the past, then, from facts, and from doctrines, Schweitzer turned to the living present spirit of Christ at work in the world. The records about Jesus were closed for the opening of association with him in a service of the natives of Africa. This was not abandonment of the study of Jesus, but the culminating stage of an apprehension of his spirit.

CHAPTER V

THE MISSIONARY

IN Schweitzer's boyhood the afternoon services at the Günsbach church were devoted on the first Sunday of each month to accounts of the life and work of the missionaries. To these meetings Schweitzer attributes the awakening of his interest in missions. His first sympathy for the Negroes of Africa was aroused by a statue of Admiral Bruat at Colmar, by the sculptor Bartholdi, on which there appears the figure of a Negro whose "expression of thoughtful sadness spoke . . . of the misery of the Dark Continent."

It was not until he was thirty years of age, and well started along other lines of activity, that the idea of going to Africa as a medical missionary came to him. When twenty-one years old he had resolved to follow the pursuits of theology, philosophy, and music until he was thirty, and then to "take a path of immediate service as man to my fellow men." At the time, the nature of this service was undetermined, and the decision to go to Africa as a doctor was made, he says, only "after plans for giving other kinds of help had occupied my mind."[36]

This plan of Schweitzer's for his life had its basis in his keen sympathy with suffering, and in his sense of stewardship in any unequal enjoyment of the benefits of life. In relation to the Negro of Africa who suffers from disease, he had the conviction that, like Dives, we sin against the poor man at our gate, in that we take as a matter of course the incalculable advantages of our medical science and do not put ourselves in his place and let heart and conscience tell us what to do. This was a work of humanity which he felt needed to be recognized, and so he set about the task of medical training in order that he might personally respond to the responsibility.

The place for his work, Lambarene on the Ogowe River in Equatorial Africa, was chosen because Alsatian missionaries in the service of the Paris Evangelical Missionary Society told him of the need of a doctor there, and because the Society offered him the use of one of the mission houses at their station and gave him permission to build a hospital on their grounds. The money for the undertaking was secured by Schweitzer himself from the profits of his books and recitals. Help also came in contributions from friends. On Good Friday of 1913, having completed his preparations, he set out for this scene of his labors.

The medical work was at first beset by very serious material handicaps. Drugs required protection from climatic conditions and from insects. For a time patients had to be treated in the open air; and then it became necessary to adapt a chicken-house to the uses of a surgery. But despite these difficulties sufferers from sleeping sickness, hernia, fractures, and fevers were treated without misfortune, and the reputation of the doctor grew. An intelligent native was secured as interpreter and assistant. After a time a hospital, constructed of corrugated iron and roofed with thatch, was ready. It contained two rooms thirteen feet square, and two small side rooms. Two other buildings, like large native huts, were added to serve for waiting-room and ward. In all this work of construction the doctor himself, impatient with the slowness and uncertainty of native labor, was obliged to take part not merely as foreman but as manual laborer. For the building of beds in the ward the relatives and attendants of the patients were pressed into service.

The chief ailments which Schweitzer had to treat, beyond those already mentioned, were dysentery, heart troubles, and skin diseases, with some cases of almost every disease treated by the European doctor, excepting cancer and appendicitis. One of the deepest impressions which his writings make is that of the amazing amount of illness and of the great need of medical help. "Every day thousands and thousands," he says, "endure the most terrible sufferings, though medical science could avert them."[37] One doctor with the most modest equipment, he declares, "can in a single year free from the power of suffering and death hundreds of men who must otherwise have succumbed to their fate in despair."

"What do all the disagreeable features (the meagerness of means, the exile, the unhealthful conditions) count for," he says, "compared with the joy of being here, working and helping? Just to see the joy of those who are plagued with sores, when these have been cleanly bandaged up and they no longer have to drag their poor bleeding feet through the mud, alone makes it worth while to work here."[38] In telling of a critical case which was rushed to him for operation, he says:

> How can I describe my feelings when a poor fellow is brought me in this condition? I am the only person within hundreds of miles who can help him. Because I am here and am supplied by my friends with the necessary means, he can be saved, . . . while otherwise he would have fallen a victim to the torture. This does not mean merely that I can save his life. We must all die. But that I can save him from days of torture; that is what I feel as my great and ever new privilege. Pain is a more terrible lord of mankind than even death himself.
>
> So, when the poor moaning creature comes, I lay my hand on his forehead and say to him: "Don't be afraid! In an hour's time you shall be put to sleep, and when you wake you won't feel any more pain."[39]

A deep religious interest and feeling finds expression in his letters. In the account of the above case, for example, he continues:

The operation is finished, and in the hardly lighted dormitory I watch for the sick man's awakening. Scarcely has he recovered consciousness when he stares about him and ejaculates again and again: "I've no more pain! I've no more pain!" . . . His hand feels for mine and will not let it go. Then I begin to tell him and the others who are in the room that it is the Lord Jesus who has told the doctor and his wife to come to the Ogowe, and that white people in Europe give them the money to live here and cure the sick Negroes. . . . The African sun is shining through the coffee bushes into the dark shed, but we, black and white, sit side by side and feel that we know by experience the meaning of the words, "And all ye are brethren."[40]

That the simple African is incapable of appreciating the message of Christianity, Schweitzer denies. Although the historical and doctrinal elements are almost impossible for the savage to understand, he is more reflective than is generally supposed, Schweitzer says, and he has, furthermore, an elemental experience of the meaning of salvation. Schweitzer declares:

Christianity is for him the light that shines amid the darkness of his fears; it assures him that he is not in the power of nature spirits, ancestral spirits, or fetishes, and that no human being has any sinister power over another, since the will of God really controls everything that goes on in the world.

"I lay in cruel bondage,
Thou cam'st and mad'st me free!"

These words from Paul Gerhardt's Advent hymn express better than any others what Christianity means for primitive man. That is again and again the thought that fills my mind when I take part in a service on a mission station.[41]

The most evident sympathy with the evangelistic side of mission work speaks through Schweitzer's writings. "For the work which the American missionaries began here and the French have continued," he says, "I feel a hearty admiration. It has produced among the natives human and Christian characters which would convince the most decided opponents of missions as to what the teaching of Jesus can do for primitive man."[42]

Though it is the relief of physical suffering which Schweitzer has felt as a particular duty, he is not less concerned about the spiritual woes of the native and the salvation which Christian doctrine brings to him. He says:

Within the primitive man there slumbers an ethical rationalist. He has a natural responsiveness to the notion of goodness and all that is connected with it in religion. . . . No one must think that he has described the thought-world of the Negro when he has made a full list of all the superstitious ideas which he has taken over. . . . There lives within him a dim suspicion that a correct view of what is truly good must be attainable as the result of reflection. In proportion as he becomes familiar with the higher moral ideas of the religion of Jesus, he finds utterance for something in himself that has hitherto been dumb, and something that has been tightly bound up finds release.[43]

This redemption is conceived in less theological and more ethical fashion than with many. It is, however, in its essence religious, and is a spiritual salvation which both lies in the power of the religion of Christ and constitutes the nature of Christian experience and piety.

That Schweitzer maintains his medical service in a certain degree of independence from the organized work of any religious denomination is not due to a critical attitude toward the missions or toward evangelistic Christianity. This is based in part on general independence of character, dislike for organization, doctrinal liberality, and an ability to make provision for his work outside of missionary resources. More truly, however, Schweitzer has wished to make his hospital "undenominational and international," because, as he says in a passage which brings out the deepest and most recurrent motive in his thought, "It was, and is still, my conviction that the humanitarian work to be done in the world should, for its accomplishment, call upon us as men, not as members of any particular nation or religious body."[44]

Despite his independent temperament and doctrinal liberality, we find Schweitzer, as a practical man, stressing the value of ecclesiastical organization. He thinks that Protestantism in the mission field might take a lesson from the Catholic program. Thus he remarks:

> If I had to distinguish between the aims which the two keep before them, I should say the Protestant mission puts in the first place the building up of Christian personalities, while the Catholic has in mind before all else the establishment on solid foundations of a church. The former object is the higher one, but it does not take sufficient account of realities. To make the work of training permanently successful, a firmly established

church, which grows in a natural way with the increase in the number of Christian families, is necessary.[45]

"But," he adds, "is it not the greatness of Protestantism as well as its weakness, that it means personal religion too much and church too little?"

Despite the engrossing and exacting nature of his work Schweitzer's cultural interests were not allowed to languish. He says:

> Mental work one must have, if one is to keep oneself in moral health in Africa; hence the man of culture, though it may seem a strange thing to say, can stand life in the forest better than the uneducated man, because he has a means of recreation of which the other knows nothing. When one reads a good book on a serious subject one is no longer the creature that has been exhausting itself the whole day in the contest with the unreliability of the natives and the tiresome worry of the insects; one becomes once more a man! Woe to him who does not in some such way pull himself together and gather new strength.[46]

Darkness came early, and medical treatment by lamplight was not only difficult but beset by danger of mosquitoes and of fever infection. The hours after the evening meal were devoted to the history of ethical theory and history of civilization, Schweitzer's own supply of books being supplemented through the co-operation of Professor Strohl, of the University of Zurich. There was also the organ. "The hour between lunch and the resumption of work in the hospital," he wrote in one of his letters, "is given to music, as is also Sunday afternoon."

In art, as well as in philosophical reflection, Schweitzer attributes a helpful influence to the primeval solitude and isolation. "Here too," he says, "I feel the blessing of working 'far from the madding crowd,' for there are many of J. S. Bach's organ pieces into the meaning of which I can now enter with greater ease and deeper appreciation than ever before."

On leaving Europe Schweitzer had made financial provision for his work for two years. Additional contributions kept coming in, and it was possible to continue the work for two and a half years longer. But drugs and supplies were used more rapidly than was expected, and meanwhile the war brought hardships. Trade and industry on the Ogowe stopped. Food was scarce. Schweitzer was cut off from Strassburg, and with that from the replenishment of materials and funds. Finally, in 1917, already in debt for the continuance of the work, depleted of stores, and with the health of his wife and himself impaired, he was obliged to go back to Europe.

To lay the foundation for return to Africa was very difficult. Many of the supporters of the hospital had been reduced to poverty by the war, and they were divided by national feeling. That he might discharge debts incurred for the earlier work it was necessary to secure funds through lectures and recitals. In the face of such unfavorable conditions, rising prices meant heavier cost for supplies. Two operations were necessary to restore Schweitzer's health; and that of his wife was such as to make her return unsafe.

But the difficulties were faced and overcome. In the beginning of 1924, although obliged to leave his wife in Europe, Schweitzer again set sail for Lambarene. He was accompanied only by an eighteen-year-old Oxford student of chemistry, who helped him during the first difficult months and until other assistance came.

It was the middle of April, 1924, when Schweitzer and his companion arrived at Lambarene, after a slow trip along the coast. The return, unaccompanied by his wife, to the scene of their former labors, which, he says, he had many times despaired of ever seeing again, moved him profoundly.

There was no delay in beginning work, although it was noon of the Saturday before Easter. The condition of his buildings can be seen in his graphic description:

> The place is a setting for the Sleeping Beauty. Grass and underbrush are growing on the sites of the buildings which I erected with such labor. The corrugated iron shed which contains the operating room, the clinic and the dispensary, is still standing, and also one of the huts for the accommodation of the sick. These two buildings are fairly well preserved, except that their thatched roofs are in a hopeless condition.[47]

The roofs were the objects of chief concern. The missionaries on the station had kept them in some degree of repair for a considerable time, but had been obliged to give up more than a year before, on account of difficulty in securing the thatches of plaited leaves. Because of the postwar demand for lumber in Europe and America all the natives were working on timber in the woods or on the river, "and no one had thought for months of such a thing as plaiting thatches of palm leaves and bamboo."

With the broken roofs it was impossible to set out materials or to begin work, and within three hours of his arrival Schweitzer was hunting through the native villages for thatches. He returned with just sixty-four, barely enough for patching the worst holes. "What I paid in flattery and presents to carry away those sixty-four thatches, I prefer to forget," he says: "I even resorted to threats, if I was not satisfied at any place, that I would never treat another patient from that particular village, but these were received with amusement as the jests of 'our doctor.'"[48] With these limited materials, and with the help of five workmen and an overseer who were placed at his disposal by a native lumberman, the dispensary and clinic were quickly made usable.

The next greatest need was a new roof for the ward. Patients had begun to arrive on Easter Monday, and they had to be lodged there, although it was the rainy season and they were obliged to lie on the ground, where they were drenched whenever there were heavy storms. Two hundred more thatches had been secured—but thousands were needed. Tiresome trips were made up and down stream. "So many afternoons which are sorely needed for care of the sick or to put affairs in order," Schweitzer lamented, "have to be spent in a canoe searching for plaited leaves!"[49]

It was about a month and a half before the roof of the main ward was in a reasonably good state of repair. Then there was need of more thatches for the roofs of the corrugated iron hospital building, the doctor's house, and other buildings which were erected. Tallies of thatches mingled with accounts of treatments on almost every page of the report for the first half year. By October he wrote:

> My moral principles are actually beginning to deteriorate. Just as when I was a boy I asked every aunt who came on visit whether she had brought along a present for me, so now I am asking for thatches and such things from everyone with whom I have anything to do. It is my dream

that sometime I shall have finished building and shall be able to be simply a physician again, that I shall not need to be exacting thatches any longer, that it will not be necessary any more for me to be a taskmaster who routs the people out from their stew-kettles to work, and who must know and thwart all their tricks to escape their stint of labor. But that day is still far in the future.[50]

It was not only that roofs had to be repaired, but beds had to be constructed, shelves and closets fashioned, bricks made and dried, and new wards built. Almost the only labor available was that of patients who were strong enough to work, or of relatives and friends who had accompanied them and who by gifts and various compulsions could be induced to work. Close oversight had always to be kept by Schweitzer himself, and much of the actual work fell to his own hands. He was obliged to divide himself between medical work and building. The latter too was made more arduous by difficulties in securing necessary materials. Excursions had to be made into the forests and swamps for bamboo; boards and beams were almost unobtainable; and large canoes and gangs of workmen were not available when wanted. Even in October he says:

What I have secured thus with such great effort and high cost has been only enough for patchwork and for the roof of a new ward. The urgently needed replacement of the roofs of my dwelling and of the corrugated iron building which contains the operating room and dispensary must be given up, and on that account I look forward with great apprehension to the stormy season.[51]

In the meantime, however, he had been joined by a nurse; and with the arrival of the river steamer, in the middle of October, came another doctor as assistant. With these valuable acquisitions at his disposal he wrote, in great relief:

The help came in the nick of time. I could not have carried for another day longer the double burden of builder and physician. What have I not suffered, because so many calls upon the sick, which ought to have been undertaken, were not made, for the reason that neither time nor energy, even by the most intense effort, was adequate! And what mental pain has it not caused me, that in cases of vigorous and dangerous treatment such as so many of the tropical diseases require, I was not able to see the patient frequently enough! How often should the microscope and the test tube have been consulted, when they were not! In surgery also only the most urgent cases were undertaken.[52]

The assistance meant "release from the torture of medical practice which was of necessity too superficial." Further, the relief in spirit from the too great single responsibility for the sick and for the practical work of the hospital was great. He wrote, "It came to me like an experience of rapture to be able to admit to myself how tired I am."

From the first the pressure of medical work was heavy. Schweitzer found cases of sleeping sickness and leprosy so prevalent as to indicate an increase in these evils since his first residence in Lambarene. The sleeping sickness, spread by mobilization of natives as troops and carriers, had seriously depleted the resident population. Among the natives who pressed from the interior to take their places and the gangs brought from inland by lumbermen to work in the timber of the Ogowe forests and swamps, dysentery, malaria, and "eating sores" of the feet made great ravages. During the first stay in Lambarene about forty patients were on hand at a time; now there were about a hundred and twenty.

In the spring of 1925 a third doctor came, to help especially with the surgery; and in the fall of the same year, a second nurse. On the arrival of the second doctor a three-room house had been built for him and for some of the white patients, of whom from two to twelve were always on hand, and by whom the capacity of the house first allotted to the doctor had been seriously overtaxed. Then an additional seven rooms had to be added for these patients and for storage space. Finally the hospital, with its several buildings, and with its over a hundred and twenty patients and their relatives, was too much for the limited quarters of the mission station, and the transfer of the hospital to a larger, independent site two miles upstream was undertaken. The buildings had been constructed in the first place with a view to their possible removal, but the task was an enormous one; and Schweitzer had to relinquish until 1927 a visit to Europe which he had planned for the fall of 1925.

Apart from the distraction from medical work occasioned by the practical work of building, Schweitzer's chief trials in the second period in Africa were due to the undisciplined character of the patients, and to the almost uncontrollable spread of dysentery.

The patients during the first period had been residents of the section; they were now wild blacks from the interior who were brought in as transient workers. Different dialects were represented (sometimes as many as fifteen), and with some of the patients no communication was possible. These almost primitive savages had no sense of ownership, and stole from each other, from the mission and from the hospital with equal lack of regard. In a large percentage of cases they had little or no feeling of gratitude. Most trying of all, they could not be brought to observe the simplest and most directly commanded sanitary precautions.

In the regulation of these matters no reliance could be placed on the native hospital helpers, since they neither exercised any authority nor attempted to do so; but a constant, and often vain, vigilance by the doctors was demanded. If the patients were present for any length of time, they became trained to a certain amount of discipline, but they were always being replaced by new arrivals with whom a fresh start had to be made.

In spite of the aid of his new assistants,

and of the re-enforcement of spirits which their arrival brought, Schweitzer writes, in a way that is without precedent in his earlier letters, of fatigue, illness, and nervous strain:

> Through the constantly growing epidemic of dysentery the work in the hospital becomes ever more difficult. All of us are exhausted and discouraged. Our attempts to halt the contamination of the hospital are in vain. Already several patients, who came to us on account of other diseases, have contracted dysentery here, and some of them could not be saved. . . .
>
> We worry ourselves to death to enforce quarantine in the hospital, but all in vain. . . . The lack of understanding of that kind of thing among our savages makes all our efforts futile. . . . One day, in despair over folks who had repeatedly contaminated the water, I dropped on a stool in the consultation-room and exclaimed, "What a fool I am, that I have tried to be doctor to such savages!" Softly Joseph murmured, "Yes, on earth you are a big fool, but not in heaven."[53]

Schweitzer's highly characteristic comment on the remark of his native helper was: "He is fond of sententious sayings, but I only wish he would support us better in our measures against the spread of dysentery."

In their concern about nails, the sawing of timbers, the hunting of bamboo, and the recovery of drifted canoes, Schweitzer's communications remind one of *Robinson Crusoe*. More noteworthy, however, is their resemblance to the letters of Paul; though it is not the resourceful Paul in perils on land and sea of whom one is most reminded, despite the community at those points, but the Paul of sharp transitions from reproof to rejoicing, from practical affairs to spiritual interests. The monotonous and wearying concern with daily chores and difficulties is broken by joy over the healing of a case of sleeping sickness taken early in its course, the successful outcome of a difficult operation, or the saving of a badly infected arm. A chief, whose shattered hand has been saved, forgets the sorely needed thatches he has promised, but Schweitzer concludes, "In spite of that, I hold him in friendly remembrance." A youth who has proved to be a valuable assistant in building leaves him in time of need, but after a passage as crisp as that of Paul about Mark, Schweitzer adds, "Despite the distress which he occasioned me, I have a high regard for him." When a patient slipped away before a cure was completed, he laments, "All my efforts and all my expenditures were thereby made of no avail!" but promptly continues:

> In contrast to such discouraging cases many are to be found which fill one with satisfaction. As a rule, the sick and their relatives are genuinely grateful. It is only that I must not count too much on any practical expressions of that gratitude.[54]

One wonders at the spirit in which the work is carried on! What is its source, and what is its support?

Schweitzer is imposed upon in the feeding of the sick and their attendants, and in the care of the aged and hopelessly ill who have no relatives. The native stands by with complete indifference and declines help where he and his relatives are not concerned, or, when he has been taught to read and write, where manual labor is involved. While dysentery rages, the wild transient from the interior dips water from the river rather than go a few steps farther to the spring, and cooks and eats from the same bowl with the sick, if vigilance is relaxed for the briefest time. He has no idea of value, but with utter unconcern wastes and destroys valuable medical supplies about whose care he has been

over

strictly admonished. He steals the fruit and the chickens of the mission station without conscience. He cannot be depended upon to present himself at the dispensary for his treatments, but must be hunted and brought there by the arm.

In the face of these dispiriting difficulties, of the unceasing stream of illness, of the heedless and irresponsible attitude of the patients, of the lack of gratitude, and of the indifference of the African to the needs of his fellows, effort is sustained; devotion and joy in the work do persist. For every case of suffering and woe, no matter what the circumstances, Schweitzer has fresh sympathy. Toward these wild and undisciplined natives who make their own relief so difficult, and who are so unresponsive, he shows unfailing compassion and love. How he is affected by their woes he indicates:

> What a sad spectacle it is when these emaciated people, whose features immediately proclaim them to be savages from the interior, are set down at the hospital with their meager bundles. No matter how often one may have observed it, one cannot fail to be touched afresh by this misery. An inexpressible sympathy for the poor stranger grips one. And how often it is hopeless sympathy,

since it is apparent at the first glance that the new arrival will draw his last breath here, far from his kin who await his return and the money which he is to bring with him.[55]

In the press of work, anxiety, difficulties, and unresponsiveness, Schweitzer never loses his sense of humanity and of the reality and poignancy of its spiritual experiences.

The medical work of Albert Schweitzer among the blacks of Africa is more than a mere biographical fact. It is the conclusion of a spiritual process which had its beginnings in *The Philosophy of Religion of Kant* and developed through *The Quest of the Historical Jesus* to this result. Each feature in the intellectual history of Schweitzer had its essential place in this development; and, taken together, his studies and their results led to his humanitarian activity as inevitably as the premises of a syllogism to their conclusion.

The conception of Schweitzer as a left-wing higher critic which was created by *The Quest of the Historical Jesus* has begun to be questioned. A fellow missionary remarks that, while he evidently still adheres to the central result of that writing, he has counted everything but loss that he might be true to his vision of the Christ. Again the same writer declares:

> In a very outstanding degree this man's thought and his life are one; . . . no discerning reader of his recent books can fail to perceive that his self-dedication to medical work among the neglected is the morally fitting expression of his whole outlook on life and God and duty.[56]

CHAPTER VI

THE PHILOSOPHER

"THE owl of Minerva," Hegel observed, "flies by night." That is to say, a philosophy first appears in practical expression, and only as the final step of its development, secures conscious rational representation. A spiritual reality which exists first as original and creative impulse must pass through the stage of externalization in objective fact before it rises to the level of conscious self-knowledge in the form of idea. Experience bears out this insight of Hegel's repeatedly in education and in history: practical action appears as an integral part of the knowing process, and a conscious knowledge of its own fundamental principles comes to an individual or to a civilization not before they have been realized in life, but afterward. It is, at any rate, in accordance with this principle that the spiritual development of Schweitzer has proceeded and has culminated in a philosophy of civilization. In his sacrificial activity his ethical philosophy secured reality and confirmation, and in his philosophy his activity attained unity and completeness. His philosophy presents the principle which interprets the antecedent events of his life and constitutes their integrity.

The first exposition of Schweitzer's philosophy of civilization was in lectures given at the University of Upsala and at Oxford in the years when he was in Europe regaining strength and support for the restoration of his hospital at Lambarene.[57] How he had been engaged in this line of thought during his university career and in the midst of his medical labors in Africa, is recounted in the preface of the English edition and in a letter of the date of Christmas, 1915. He wrote of his daily routine in Africa:

> If the day has not been too exhausting I can give a couple of hours after supper to my studies in ethics and civilization as part of the history of human thought. . . . Strange indeed are the surroundings amid which I study; my table stands inside the lattice door which leads on the verandah, so that I may snatch as much as possible of the light evening breeze. The palms rustle an obligato to the loud music of the crickets and the

toads, and from the forest come harsh and terrifying cries of all sorts. . . . In this solitude I try to set in order thoughts which have been stirring in me since 1900, in the hope of giving some little help to the restoration of civilization. Solitude of the primeval forest, how can I ever thank you enough for what you have been to me?[58]

Schweitzer, in common with Spengler and many other European thinkers, is convinced that modern civilization fails to embody features of permanent significance for man, and that its decay is in process.[59] He takes this as almost self-evident, and considers that the business of thoughtful men is not to prove the fact, but to diagnose the causes. The only reason we can fail to see this clearly and universally is that we have been misled by a striking advance in mechanical power and material prosperity. This is a phenomenon which has never before occurred except in conjunction with an intellectual and moral advance. Our satisfaction with it has led us to overlook the fact that such development is not in itself an advance in civilization, and that in this case it was not accompanied by that ethical spirit which is the basis and content of genuine civilization. Only when our civilization began to crumble for want in general thought of any rational convictions which would serve to maintain ethical conduct, did it become apparent to some that our civilization was bankrupt and in process of collapse.

Schweitzer explicitly rejects the easy-going faith in progress which has associated itself with the theory of evolution. To him, the course of natural processes and the realization of genuine civilization are two distinct and unrelated things. This idea of an inexorable evolutionary development is, he says, a "despiritualized optimism about reality which has for decades been misleading us."[60] We enjoy a false confidence "as if the contradictions which show themselves in the world arranged themselves automatically so as to promote well-thought-out progress, and reconciled themselves in syntheses in which the valuable parts of the thesis and antithesis coalesced,"[61] and shun the true alternative, that genuine progress in civilization depends upon the power of ethical ideas which are arrived at by reason and supported by the activity of the ethical spirit.

A recognition of the defects and evils of

civilization is urgently needed. Any hope for the renewal of civilization depends upon a consciousness of the absolute indefensibility of the material and spiritual conditions under which we live, that is, upon an apprehension of the character of what *is* and of what *ought to be,* in their contrast.

The disproportionate attention given to our material progress, and the conditions of life with which that material progress has been associated, have confused us in regard to the true nature of civilization and robbed us of the opportunity and power of reflection about it. While the material progress of society is an element in civilization, it is not an unqualified element nor the essential one. The essence of civilization is ethical; it lies in the development of the motive to raise life, in so far as we can determine it, to its highest degree of value. It is this element, Schweitzer believes, which has been decaying in our Western world. Our society is characterized by lack of freedom, over-organization, subjugation of the individual mind to group thought, and indifference toward human life and sensibilities. So, even while the wave of material progress has risen to its crest, the essential factor of civilization has been on the decline, and civilization has no longer either creative vigor or endurance.

The essential reason for the plight of our civilization is its lack of a rationally defensible world-view as foundation for the ethical ideals upon whose operation in society its soundness is dependent. During the period of Rationalism the ethical ideals which are necessary to civilization were supported by a living, popular philosophy that interpreted reality in such a way as to find meaning in it for human life and values, and to maintain enthusiasm for civilization. But that naïve and dogmatic metaphysic, in spite of the support it had for a time from Kant and Hegel, fell under the criticism of pure thought, and the popular mind was left without a rational set of ideas which would put conviction and enthusiasm behind ethical purposes and activity.

Philosophy, it is true, undertook the task of replacing the ridiculed metaphysical structure of Rationalism by an interpretation of the world which would be more empirical and in closer accord with the findings of the natural sciences; but in doing so it lost touch with human values and neglected its real duty. Its obligation was to maintain civilization by putting into general circulation a secure philosophical outlook which would engender enthusiasm and activity in the advancement of life.

Philosophy further betrayed civilization, Schweitzer asserts, by cherishing the view that such an optimistic and ethical outlook could be based on our interpretation of the world. The failure of pure thought to secure an optimistic and ethical outlook for life in this way is not the fault of philosophy, Schweitzer thinks; but it is a fact which it might be expected to have recognized and admitted.

Schweitzer regards the optimistic-ethical world- and life-attitude which has been a constant trait of Occidental theory as its distinctive characteristic. The West presents only this one world-attitude, in distinction from the alternative world-view of the Orient, which is that of resignation and world-negation. Our philosophical systems have all alike had the one aim of giving a rational basis to the ethical attitude, and we have tenaciously clung to these systems even when they were found to be faulty. Temporarily some of them, among these notably eighteenth-century Rationalism, succeeded in giving support to our ideals, and stimulated civilization; but ultimately each system revealed defects to pure thought, and ceased to command the conviction which made it a civilizing power. Thus Schweitzer considers that philosophy has left our ethical attitude toward life without rational grounds, and sees the history of philosophy, which he reviews in the second volume of the *Philosophy of Civilization,* as the tragedy of the Occidental world-view.

The scientific merit of the methods of modern philosophy of nature is not questioned by Schweitzer, nor the general soundness of its results, but only its relative importance in the comprehensive business of philosophy. Philosophy has been too engrossed with its idea of solving the mysteries of the universe, he thinks, and too confident that when it did this it would find its ethical ideals grounded there. It has been oblivious to the fact that the ethical elements in our civilization have been perishing while it has been holding out an empty hope of a scientifically established metaphysics which would lay their foundation in objective reality.

There are several objections to the program which philosophy has set for itself. One is that the demands of optimistic activity cannot brook the delay and uncertainty of a metaphysical foundation which, as empirical, is never final. Another is that it is not (Socrates to the contrary) the purely rational element of understanding which gives impulse and direction to conduct, but nonrational factors. Finally, there is no antecedent assurance that metaphysical inquiry, if it could be assumed to arrive at a final world-interpretation, would offer the help to human life and value that is sought.

Schweitzer declares:

> My own solution of the problem is that we must make up our minds to renounce altogether any optimistic-ethical interpretation of the world. . . . Our knowledge of the world is unable to furnish us with any data on which to base either world- and life-affirmation or ethics. . . . Our progress in knowledge consists solely in the fact that we are able to describe the phenomena which make up the objective world, together with their issues, with ever greater detail and accuracy. It is impossible for us to comprehend the meaning

of the whole—and yet our concern for a world-view has no other object than this.[62]

Thus, with general disillusionment about the worth of our mechanical and material progress Schweitzer combines denial that our scientific knowledge is directly or necessarily a step toward the attainment of genuine progress, and that it gives any assurance of unity of the actual and the ethical.

To renounce the attempt to interpret the objective world in such a light as to find in it meaning for human life and for its aims does not mean to Schweitzer, however, a renunciation of the optimistic and ethical world-attitude. He says of himself, "I think I am the first Western thinker who has dared to acknowledge as truth this crushing intellectual conclusion, and to be absolutely skeptical with regard to our knowledge of the objective world, without at the same time renouncing world- and life-affirmation and ethics."[63] It is Schweitzer's theory, and a distinctive principle of his philosophy, that the basis of such an attitude is not to be sought in knowledge of the world, but is to be rationally deduced from the facts of ethical volition. His view is that the "will-to-live," by which he does not mean an instinct of self-preservation but a will to preserve and to advance all life, can not only stand by itself, but can support a philosophical system instead of resting upon one. What our civilization needs in order to be living and progressive is respect for life, not founded upon an uncertain interpretation of the world but upon our will to live and to perfect life, and upon recognition of the will in all life.

The ground of man's hope for a perfection of civilization, and of his enthusiasm for life, cannot be a rational one, according to Schweitzer. The actual world offers no warrant for such hopes and enthusiasm; and they are not justified by any presentation of evidence for them. They spring from the "will-to-live" itself, and depend upon it.

The actual world does not furnish our ethical ideals, but, to the contrary, they demand that it conform to them. That we have looked more or less to reality to produce progress independent of the human effort to work out ethical ideas by reason and to incorporate them in reality has been a source of ethical weakness. We are not to depend upon some interpretation of the world to give human values a significant metaphysical position, but to trust directly and immediately in the optimistic-ethical will.

The value of conscious life has to be accepted without rational reason for it, either religious or philosophical. It is involved in the will-to-live, and without demonstration to reason it is adopted by the ethical will as its controlling principle. The respect for life is thus founded not upon beliefs, but upon a volition. It is in itself nonrational, but it is the attitude, Schweitzer says, which reason discovers and justifies. True rationalism is eventually mysticism. It leads to and builds from an experience in which the individual accepts and identifies himself with a universal WILL-to-Live.

CHAPTER VII

SCHWEITZER'S CONTRIBUTIONS

SCHWEITZER'S *Quest of the Historical Jesus* is a book, Reinhold Niebuhr says, "through which all New Testament criticism was profoundly affected."[64] But that the theological views contained in it are fully acceptable either to Christian feeling or to Christian scholarship in general is not to be expected. The conceptions of the life of Jesus and of the course of religious progress presented by it are both too individual and too vigorous, and too much at odds with our familiar ways of thought and our traditional religious values, to be either readily favored or compromised with. In the suggestion that eschatological expectations not only entered into the thought of Jesus, but even played the determinative part in his message and ministry, Schweitzer introduced something new into the field of New Testament criticism.[65] It is precisely on this theory, further, that opposition to eschatological interpretations centers. Though it was at one time the fashion to reject or weaken all the eschatological passages in the sayings of Jesus, theologians now readily admit that Jesus' expressions were colored by the view. What they will not accept is that his ministry was guided by these ideas and that our conception of a developing ethical and spiritual kingdom did not belong to him. For Schweitzer, however, these are the main facts which emerge from the research.

That Schweitzer is too consistent in his application of the eschatological principle is a criticism commonly made. His unvarying reference to this one principle of explanation for the life and teachings of Jesus seems to carry the theory too far. To many of his interpretations, as both Wernle and Holtzmann remark, one might reply in his own oft-repeated phrase, "But there is nothing of that in the text."

It is not necessary to the theory, of course, to maintain that every incident in the recorded life of Jesus is explained by his eschatological expectations. Schweitzer himself observes that many things are to be attributed to Jesus' sympathy and to his ethical earnestness unaffected by eschatological considerations. In his expositions, however, he seems to forget this and to go farther in the application of this single principle of explanation than the theory requires or the material justifies.

Schweitzer believes that the eschatological theory makes the great body of incidents in the ministry of Jesus intelligible, and that it offers solution of the most stubborn problems of critical research. That it does both of these things with considerable plausibility can scarcely be denied. The reader cannot escape the impression of how naturally and adequately it explains Jesus' "hard sayings," and of how simply it takes care of incidents which are difficult for the rationalistic view. These features in the relation of the theory to the sources are too pronounced to credit them, with Jülicher, wholly to the "marvelous . . . art with which the author weaves his strange fabric out of threads of old tradition."

Whether the issue between Schweitzer's consistently eschatological life of Jesus and the liberal life of Jesus developed by rationalistic theology can be conclusively settled can be determined only through extensive work on the sources by unbiased specialists. There is apparent so much, however: first, that the theory has made it impossible for critical theology to be dogmatic in its liberal picture of Jesus, and has required it to validate its results; and secondly, that for Schweitzer himself the "convictions he has either learned from or been confirmed in by his study of the historical Jesus . . . are nothing less than a releasing or redeeming gospel."

The figure of Jesus which Schweitzer discovered in his attempt to be faithful to the sources and to exclude the influence of our own ethical humanism was largely strange and unintelligible. This Jesus did not belong to a common realm of thought with us, and seemed to be without meaning for us in our different outlook. Disillusionment about the relation of our moral ideas and program to the mind of Jesus was the fruit of the eschatological view. But through this outcome Schweitzer found, as the thing of central significance in Jesus, the presence of an ethical spirit which distinguished itself from the world and sought to spiritualize it.

This active moral will was found as a positive spiritual and spiritualizing element in his world and in ours.

To the problems of philosophy Schweitzer comes with the rather unusual qualifications of a co-ordinate high development of the academic, æsthetic and practical activities of the human spirit. These are not the common credentials of a professional philosopher, but in Schweitzer we must recognize the claims made by an outstanding and vigorous personality whose varied activities are not merely diverse pursuits but a coherent spiritual expression.

Philosophical speculation has been entered upon by various thinkers for different ends—to satisfy religious thought, to secure and justify universal laws in science, or to found morality. The last is Schweitzer's purpose. For him, further, it is ethical experience whose consideration forms the chief business of philosophical thought and whose analysis secures the content of philosophical knowledge.

Vigorous attack upon materialistic and utilitarian principles in individual and social life is made in Schweitzer's writings. He recognizes material progress as an element in civilization, and regards the establishment of favorable conditions of living as desirable both for its own sake and for its contribution to the spiritual and moral progress of individuals. He does not, however, consider these things as of the essence of civilization. The measure of civilization is taken, not by its artistic, scientific, and material treasures, but by the amount and vigor of its ethical will.

The nature of the ethical spirit and of ethical activity is that they are dominated by the attitude of affirmation of life, and that they are devoted to the preservation and advancement of life. The extent of reference of their principle of reverence for life is unlimited. Not even at the border of animal life, Schweitzer thinks, does responsibility toward life end. The ethical man does not ask how far any form of life is capable of feeling, but to him life as such is sacred; he "tears no leaf from its tree, breaks off no flower" without being forced to do so by necessity and then only with a bad conscience.[66] "The good conscience is an invention of the devil."

Such a principle of reverence for life inevitably involves personal sacrifice. To realize fully what is implicit in the will toward life and to make it perfect, simple life-affirmation must include in itself an element of life-negation.[67]

Logical limits are not to be set up for either the life-affirmation or correlative voluntary life-negation. When normal and unimpaired, they express the subjective enthusiasm for life. Where they are governed by objective considerations and rules, it is a sign of weakening of the ethical will.[68]

Schweitzer's ethics dispenses with utilitarian considerations. Ethical conduct is not that action which is seen to be necessary for certain practical ends, and it is not decided by anticipation of its consequences or by its hopes of success. To be ethical is merely to surrender oneself wholly to the behest of the subjective impulse of reverence for life unweakened by theoretical considerations.

It is out of an inner constraint, according to Schweitzer, not out of prudent accommodation to the world, that morality arises. It has its source in the experience of the will-to-live when it has thought itself out completely and has actualized the world-affirmation inherent in it.[69]

In this experience in one's own person of an active reverence for life Schweitzer believes that the true nature of reality is discovered. Every reality, he thinks, is a manifestation of creative will toward the realization of life and the fulfillment of its inherent possibilities. We experience as an intrinsic part of our being, he says, an impulse "to raise ourselves and every portion of existence affected by our influence to the highest material and spiritual degree of value";[70] and through this experience of reality which we have in ourselves, we understand reality as power—further, as a power that acts purposively; and, more fully, as a "power determined by ideals."[71]

This outlook is not—and Schweitzer thinks it cannot be—a theoretical conclusion from facts of the natural world. It goes beyond anything which observation of them either suggests or confirms. In the way of study of the world of nature, no comprehension of the inner principle of reality can be obtained; but this impossibility is not a thing which leads to skepticism, but "the very truth which we must dare to grasp in order to find in it that world-view of which we dream. . . ." Schweitzer surrenders the hope of securing for philosophical belief a consistent system of subjective and objective appearances, and accepts the experience of reality in our own spirits as the clearest and best-established knowledge of it.[72]

Schweitzer's method involves a reversal of the course which philosophy has consistently tried to pursue. The attempt has been to discover theoretically a meaning in the natural world which would make life supremely and permanently significant. Indian philosophy concluded that this was impossible, resigned the optimistic world-attitude, and developed an ethics of apathy and resignation. Western philosophy, on the other hand, persisted in the quest, courageously and ingeniously, but with uncertain success. Sometimes it has surrendered intellectual vigor and sincerity in order to find its ideals in the world, and sometimes it has lowered its ethics to the place where the natural dominated the ideal instead of the reverse.

The supposition that the way to a general theory of life must be through metaphysics, Schweitzer rejects as a mistake. To regard the theory of the natural world as the parent of a philosophy of life, he says, is a reversal of the true relation. An interpretation of the world must have its origin in the actively optimistic attitude to life.[73]

That reality is will-toward-the-furtherance-of-life appears in Schweitzer's system in the first place not as a deduction, but as a fact of immediate experience. Schweitzer desires a world-view created by rational reflection, but holds that the most clear and primary datum for thought is a nonrational impulse. The service of reflection is to discover this disposition as its starting-point, and to encourage an expression and experience of reality in its normal form.

There are very definite elements of mysticism in Schweitzer's thought. It is not the world of objects, but the inner experience of life which is the primary philosophical fact. Through it all merely intellectual knowledge is transcended in the senses that knowledge is achieved where pure intellect would remain in ignorance, and that the character of reality beyond oneself is not merely recognized but directly experienced. This reality is comprehended not through extensive observation of its manifestations, but through sympathetic intuition of the inner principle of its being. Through such a comprehension the individual can make the purposes of the reality beyond himself in some degree his own, and achieve unity of will with it. By this activity, then, the truth of the interpretation can be verified.

The last idea indicates that part of Schweitzer's mysticism can be identified with the sound, experimental side of pragmatism. Knowledge itself is viewed as incomplete until it has been venturesomely tried in action. It is not the function of a pure intellect, but of the whole man; and will, in the form of action, has to do its part. Only if one obeys life's inherent impulse does one learn and reveal what the nature of life really is, namely, will to preserve and enhance life. The will-to-live calls, as Jesus did, for service in advance of understanding; and here too some persons (not the "little-faiths, true followers of Peter," who "cry out and sink in the sea of ideas," but "the followers of Paul, who believe in the Spirit") follow in the ethical venture of faith and then as an ineffable secret they experience what Life is.

The influences which contributed to the production of Schweitzer's philosophy were wide and varied. He has a comprehensive knowledge of the forms and history of philosophical thought, and his relations to philosophers and systems are diverse—often very significant, but always free.[74] Kant and Schopenhauer influenced him most. He derived something from Nietzsche, from Bergson, and from Hegel. There are affinities to Leibnitz and to William Stern. But the first place among the factors which determined his view must be given to his own traits and temperament.

The ready and intense feeling of sympathy for the experiences—the joys and the sufferings—of all living things which is prominent in Schweitzer's philosophy has its chief source in his personal disposition. Æsthetic sensibility contributes something. To some extent the respect for crystal, flower, and insect is born from an ability to see and to thrill at the perfection of line and of proportion in them. In even greater measure, however, it arises from the closely allied, but not primarily æsthetic feeling of sympathy. In the stories of his childhood Schweitzer tells that the cries of pain of a dog which he had struck with a whip haunted him for weeks, that the sound of the church bell, as if a voice from heaven commanding "Thou shalt not kill," had led him to scare away from a friend's sling the birds which they had been stalking, and that fishing was impossible for him because of the treatment of the worms and the tearing of the fishes' mouths. One might regard this as a child's squeamishness at the sight of wounds, but it is a practicing surgeon who gives the narrative, and who concludes:

From experiences like these, which moved my heart and often made me feel ashamed, there slowly grew up in me an unshakable conviction that we have no right to inflict suffering and death on another living creature unless there is some unavoidable necessity for it, and that we ought all of us to feel what a horrible thing it is to cause suffering and death out of mere thoughtlessness, and this conviction has influenced me only more and more strongly with time. I have grown more and more certain that at the bottom of our heart we all think this, and that we fail to acknowledge it and to carry our belief into practice chiefly because we are afraid of being laughed at by other people as sentimentalists, though partly also because we allow our best feelings to get blunted. But I vowed that I would never be afraid of the reproach of sentimentalism.[75]

The hardening of himself against the influence of being laughed at for sentimentality, to which Schweitzer refers, is significant. Though intense in his feelings and enthusiasms, he is at the same time reserved. Conventional restraint of the earnestness with which he has tended to throw himself into all interests, and a shyness about showing his inner life, have often led him to appear actually indifferent. It was only due to special circumstances that he was brought to allow his feeling for music to break through the "wooden playing" which he had presented to his teacher. In his religious confirmation too, as we have seen, he was the cause of deep concern to his pastor because of apparent indifference, although he says, "In reality . . . I was during those weeks so moved by the holiness of the time that I felt almost ill."[76]

His reserve about the manifestation of his feelings led Schweitzer in some few cases, such as the bird-hunting and fishing, to try at first to conceal his natural reaction. The latter triumphed in these cases, however, and afterward he came to recognize and to combat his shyness as a cause of unfaithfulness to his true nature and convictions.

The apparent callousness and indifference to suffering shown by men is originally due to their reluctance to exhibit their inner spirit, Schweitzer thinks, to fear of being considered sentimental, and to habitual hardening of natural feeling. This experience and belief form, then, the background of his insistence that subjective disposition is not to be modified by the experiences of life, or to be subjected either to external canons or to the consideration of what is rational.

The universality and democracy of Schweitzer's principle of respect for life is one of its chief characteristics. He will not so much as enter the path of classification of life as more or less valuable. Reverence for life, he says, does not ask how far any life deserves saving, but treats all life as sacred. It does not permit one to accept especial happiness or good fortune as a matter of course, or one's advantages as rights of the more worthy. In this Schweitzer carries out in wider range a protest against class distinction which he stubbornly waged in his boyhood. It distressed him that, as the pastor's son, he was placed on a different level than the village boys and was given advantages beyond theirs. Regardless of embarrassment to his parents, he would not wear any shoes except wooden clogs on week days; and since the other boys did not have overcoats, he persistently refused one. This was in part, of course, the aversion which any boy has to being different from his associates, but in Schweitzer's case it was also a protest against distinction on any conventional grounds in the consideration shown to individuals.

An ethical spirit cannot be considered a simple element in character. It is, rather, the function of sensitive sympathy, fellow feeling, and ideals. Taking it in this composite character, however, it may be said that moral disposition is the greatest personal factor in the determination of Schweitzer's philosophy. It requires a man in whom the moral impulse is the most evident and significant experience of life to build a philosophy from it in this manner. To that extent

Schweitzer's philosophy is a relative one, the expression of his own personality. The artist, or the genius in any line, however, is only an individual with somewhat heightened sensibility and insight. Without his higher development he would not be a leader, but there is also implied a common experience which he evokes and sharpens. Thus Schweitzer seeks to make men aware of and to bring to clear consciousness in them what he considers to be the fundamental experience of all men.

Whether an active spirit of regard for life is in truth an immediate, common and primary experience is a question which would call for careful and extended consideration. There are, of course, experiences of distress at the suffering of others, of empathetic sensibility in general, and of beneficent impulses. It can be claimed, on the other hand, that the sympathetic feelings and beneficent impulses are not alone in human nature, but are accompanied by contrary feelings and impulses, and that, in fact, human dispositions are as indeterminate and equivocal with respect to their moral principle as the natural world. But to this Schweitzer would reply that though this is true of them as they present themselves to external observation, and though will toward life frequently comes into conflict with itself in diverse individuals, will is revealed from within normally and universally as will toward the preservation and promotion of life, and that there is no normal will against life.

Action, of course, has a wide range of stimuli and patterns, and its objectives are varied. To say that all action has the preservation of life, or its enhancement, as its immediate object is psychologically false. It is getting this special object, or doing that particular thing, toward which the individual strives, and with the accomplishment of which he identifies himself. The particular ends are the things sought, and activity may disregard the principle of respect for life. This is responsible in large measure both for the appearance of ruthlessness which belongs to much conduct, and also for the disregard of personal interests which constitutes self-sacrifice. Still, whenever the consciousness of life and of purposive striving enters, the experience of regard for it arises.

It may then be dismissed on one ground or another, but it has been there.

There are probably persons in whom the experience is less strong than in others, just as there are individual differences in all psychological functions; but the disposition and experience may be regarded as common and normal. Objective appearances do not clearly manifest it, and there are individuals in whom it does not seem to exist, or in whom its presence seems to be contradicted. Where, however, this is not, as in the majority of cases, due to suppression of natural feelings through one type or another of self-regard or through considerations of rationality, it gives the appearance of pathological perversion of natural feeling. The power of vicious acts to catch and fixate the attention of the mentally unstable, until an impulse toward them becomes overmastering, or, in other cases, the sense of power and of self-enhancement which they give, is due to the distinctly strong impression of unnaturalness which they make.

It is as the implication of one's own will-to-live, however, even more than as that of one's sympathetic dispositions, that Schweitzer affirms the general value of life. The question of the reality of this experience then arises. Even though there is apparently more in the reaction of a living organism to the threat of death than can be accounted for by previous experience, and though there is possibly more present in consciousness in such cases than the sum of the sensory qualities, the positive assertion of an experience of some inherent force in operation for the preservation of life is not justified. If it is a question of conscious will to live, we must recognize again that the usual experience of will is of the disposition to go to some definite place, to have dinner, to make the goal in a game, or to achieve some one of a number of definite objects. On the other hand, if the matter comes in question, we shall certainly will to live. Except in the sacrificial service of life, we consider the choice not to live as a mark of ill health and mental abnormality. Moreover, the will-to-live is manifested where varied experiences, not just the saving of biological life itself, are sought. Life as a spiritual reality is the process of experiencing, and in the activity of consciousness in maintaining itself and finding content, there is experience of the will-to-live.

The experience of the will-to-live which is fundamental is undoubtedly that in the self. It is this which makes the sympathetic insight into the impulses of others and the co-operation with their purposes possible. In itself, however, it is not so narrow as the commonly-spoken-of impulse to individual self-preservation, but is a disposition of regard for life as such. It includes, together with active will to the perfecting of one's own life, spontaneous respect for other will-to-live and co-operation with its efforts. This attitude, and the conception of the value of life which it implies, do not have theoretical grounds, but are inherent in the nature of being.

Even though there are many and varied tendencies which do not directly exhibit conscious concern for life, and which in their execution come into conflict with regard for life and override it, there is considerable warrant for accepting the disposition of reverence for life as a strong and definite element of experience. Since, further, humaneness is a mark of personal and unartificial moral sense, whereas social and rational ethics sacrifices it to material considerations and to abstract principles, there is strong indication that it is innate rather than produced by social or reflective influences.

Such an innate tendency could not, however, be more than formal. Though regard for life and for its fulfillment might be considered to be the general form of action, in so far as it is determined by unspoiled inner nature, the content of each act would have to be determined in the individual case. The determination might be subjective and on the motive of respect for life, but the content of the act would represent what had been acquired through experience. For instance, Schweitzer's consciousness of the existence of life in Africa and of its needs, and his knowledge of the methods of surgery, are due to impression and to the course of experience. That which is subjective and innate is only the spirit of reverence for life in which the acts of healing are done. The innate will provides a spirit for moral action rather than a content, and it leaves the latter to be determined in experience.

Even granting, however, that the feeling of respect for life and of responsibility in relation to it is real, there remain the questions whether the fact of valuation establishes the actual value of its object, and whether the principle of one's own nature can be taken to represent reality beyond oneself. Schweitzer does not sufficiently justify the successive steps of his thought at these points,[77] but they depend ultimately on the same general faith in a conformity of the principles of our nature with those of objective reality which is a presupposition of all knowledge. This relation Schweitzer takes to be no less true of the affective and volitional principles of our nature than of the intellectual. Among equivocal appearances of life he accepts the clear and immediate experience of it in himself as representative of its true nature. This decision itself, then, represents the nature of reality, as it appears in the will. The determination of the will is not thought of as relative and capricious, but as representing a universal tendency of reality, namely, to be life-affirming. Acceptance of knowledge of any sort depends everywhere upon a similar act of faith in the objective grounds and validity of the spiritual processes.

It is deeply characteristic of Schweitzer that in the varied and seemingly conflicting representations of reality he treats the ethical impulses as the clearest revelation and the highest truth. From disheartening experiences of the world Schweitzer refuses to reach hasty conclusions about the nature of reality in general. He recognizes the features of the world which are grounds for pessimistic world-views without minimizing them, but sets them aside as insoluble mysteries, and holds on to the other fact—that convictions and ideals of self-realization and of the betterment of life arise and "carry one beyond the knowledge which our observation of the world provides."[78]

That the presence and operation of moral will in the world is taken account of seriously by Schweitzer is one of the chief merits of his thought. An adequate philosophy cannot overlook morality and its significance. It is a weakness of philosophy that in the treatment of its general problems it has been led to give less than due recognition to this factor. Schweitzer, schooled not to fear the charge of sentimentality or of tender-mindedness, performs a service for philosophical inquiry when he puts the ethical evaluations and impulses in an important place.

Even more practically serviceable than this suggestion of the theoretical significance of the ethical spirit is Schweitzer's personal manifestation of the attitude of uncalculating regard for life. The example of sacrificial service creates, or liberates, more effectively than any exposition, conviction of the worth of human life, and of the presence in it of a fundamental will directed toward the welfare of others. The faith which it generates tends to produce action in accordance with such a will and to provide cumulative evidence of its reality. Through it there is revived the confidence of men in the disposition of others to deal with them fundamentally as human beings; and the conditions of civilization, according to Schweitzer's conception of it, are secured. What Schweitzer accomplishes through this impression of his personality is his greatest contribution.

APPENDIX

The following bibliography and notes are intended merely to make acknowledgment of sources and to assist the reader who wishes to follow some idea or activity of Schweitzer's at greater length. They make no pretense either in extent or character to be the type of reference employed in a critical study. It is expected, however, that in their present form they will fully satisfy, and in the least possible degree discourage, the inquiries of the non-academic reader.

BIBLIOGRAPHY

The following works by Schweitzer are in English translation:

The Mystery of the Kingdom of God. N. Y.: Dodd, Mead and Co., 1914. London: A. & C. Black, 1925.

J. S. Bach. 2 vols. London: A. & C. Black, 1911. N. Y.: Macmillan, 1923.

The Quest of the Historical Jesus. London: A. & C. Black, 1910, 1911, 1922. N. Y.: Macmillan.

Paul and His Interpreters. London: A. & C. Black, 1912. N. Y.: Macmillan.

On the Edge of the Primeval Forest. London: A. & C. Black, 1922. N. Y.: Macmillan.

The Decay and Restoration of Civilization. London: A. &. C. Black, 1923. N. Y.: Macmillan, 1924.

Civilization and Ethics. London: A. & C. Black, 1923. N. Y.: Macmillan, 1924.

Christianity and the Religions of the World. N. Y.: G. H. Doran Co., 1923. London: Allen & Unwin, 1923.

Memoirs of Childhood and Youth. London: Allen & Unwin, 1924. N. Y.: Macmillan, 1925.

J. S. Bach's Organ-works. (With Ch. M. Widor.) N. Y.: Schirmer, 1912, 1913, 1914. Vols. I—V.

Principal works additional to the above named, but not at this time in English, are:

Die Religionsphilosophie Kants. Tübingen: J. C. B. Mohr, 1899.

Das Abendmahlsproblem auf Grund der wissenschaftlichen Forschung des 19. Jahrhunderts und der historischen Berichte. Tübingen: J. C. B. Mohr, 1901.

Deutsche und französische Orgelbaukunst und Orgelkunst. Leipzig: Breitkopf & Härtel, 1906; 2nd ed., 1927.

Die psychiatrische Beurteilung Jesu. Tübingen: J. C. B. Mohr, 1913.

Mitteilungen aus Lambarene. Drei Hefte. Bern: Paul Haupt, 1925, 1926, 1927.

Selbstdarstellung. Leipzig: Felix Meiner, 1929.

Die Mystik des Apostels Paulus. Tübingen: J. C. B. Mohr, 1929.

NOTES

[1] Ernst von Dobschütz, *Eschatology of the Gospels*, pp. 53-56.

[2] *Neue Linien*, p. 3f.

[3] *The Life of Christ in Recent Research*, p. 45f.

[4] Von Dobschütz, op. cit., p. 58.

[5] "The Apocalyptic Element in the Gospels," *Hibb. Jr.*, Oct., 1911.

[6] *Albert Schweitzer: Sein Werk und seine Weltanschauung.* Charlottenburg: Rolph Heise, 1926, p. 61.

[7] For the facts and quotations in this chapter I am indebted chiefly, with supplementation from some incidental sources, to Schweitzer's *Memoirs of Childhood and Youth* and *Selbstdarstellung.*

[8] From a biographcial note at the end of Schweitzer's doctoral dissertation, *Die religionsphilosophische Skizze der Kritik der reinen Vernunft.*

[9] From Albert Schweitzer, *Memoirs of Childhood and Youth*, p. 57f. By permission of The Macmillan Company, publishers.

[10] Ibid., p. 24. By permission of The Macmillan Company, publishers.

[11] Ibid., p. 22. By permission of The Macmillan Company, publishers.

[12] Ibid., p. 56f. By permission of The Macmillan Company, publishers.

[13] From *J. S. Bach*, I, p. vi. By permission of The Macmillan Company, publishers.

[14] From Albert Schweitzer, *Memoirs of Childhood and Youth*, p. 62. By permission of The Macmillan Company, publishers.

[15] June 18, 1912, to Helene Breslau, daughter of the Strassburg historian.

[16] Montgomery, W., *Hibb. Jr.* (1914), pp. 872-873.

[17] Mead, L. A., *Boston Herald*, Oct. 26, 1927.

[18] Dr. Von Müller, *Westermann's Monatshefte*, 140 (1926), p. 309.

[19] For this discussion of art by Schweitzer see the *Memoirs of Childhood and Youth*, p. 96, and *J. S. Bach*, II, pp. 8, 13.

[20] See *J. S. Bach*, II, p. 468.

[21] From Albert Schweitzer, *The Quest of the Historical Jesus*, p. 397. By permission of The Macmillan Company, publishers.

[22] Ibid., p. 238.

[23] Ibid., p. 238f., p. 363.

[24] Ibid., p. 281f.

[25] Ibid., p. 239.

[26] Ibid., p. 87, et al.

[27] From Albert Schweitzer, *Paul and His Interpreters*, p. 238. Cf. p. 186. By permission of The Macmillan Company, publishers.

[28] Ibid., p. 249. Cf. 193f. By permission of The Macmillan Company, publishers.

[29] See Ibid., pp. 215-225.

[30] Ibid., p. 249. Cf. p. 194. By permission of The Macmillan Company, publishers.

[31] From Albert Schweitzer, *The Quest of the Historical Jesus*, p. 400. By permission of The Macmillan Company, publishers.

[32] *Die psychiatrische Beurteilung Jesu.*

[33] Schweitzer's dissertation for the degree of doctor of medicine, *Kritik der von medezinischer Seite veröffentlichten Pathographien über Jesus*, p. 43.

[34] See *The Quest of the Historical Jesus*, p. 396.

[35] From Albert Schweitzer, *The Quest of the Historical Jesus*, p. 401. By permission of The Macmillan Company, publishers.

[36] See the *Memoirs of Childhood and Youth*, p. 83, *Selbstdarstellung*, p. 18.

[37] From Albert Schweitzer, *On the Edge of the Primeval Forest*, p. 171. By permission of The Macmillan Company, publishers.

[38] Ibid., p. 37. By permission of The Macmillan Company, publishers.

[39] Ibid., p. 92. By permission of The Macmillan Company, publishers.

[40] Ibid., p. 93. By permission of The Macmillan Company, publishers.

[41] Ibid., p. 154. By permission of The Macmillan Company, publishers.

[42] Ibid., p. 167. By permission of The Macmillan Company, publishers.

[43] Ibid., p. 155. By permission of The Macmillan Company, publishers.

[44] Ibid., p. 3. By permission of The Macmillan Company, publishers.

[45] Ibid., p. 166f. By permission of The Macmillan Company, publishers.

[46] Ibid., p. 149. By permission of The Macmillan Company, publishers.

[47] *Mitteilungen aus Lambarene*, I, p. 20.

[48] Ibid., p. 21.

[49] Ibid., p. 22.

[50] Ibid., p. 43.

[51] Ibid., p. 44.

[52] *Mitteilungen aus Lambarene*, II, p. 3.

[53] Ibid., p. 56f.

[54] *Mitteilungen aus Lambarene*, I, p. 28.

[55] *Mitteilungen aus Lambarene*, II, p. 114.

[56] Hogg, A. G., *International Review of Missions*, 14 (1925), p. 47.

[57] Published as *The Philosophy of Civilization:* Vol. I, *The Decay and Restoration of Civilization;* Vol. II, *Civilization and Ethics.*

[58] From Albert Schweitzer, *On the Edge of the Primeval Forest*, p. 148f. By permission of The Macmillan Company, publishers.

[59] He is apparently not influenced by Spengler, however, and his viewpoint is wholly different.

[60] *The Decay and Restoration of Civilization*, p. 39.

[61] Loc. cit.

[62] From Albert Schweitzer, *Civilization and Ethics, p. xii.* By permission of The Macmillan Company, publishers.

[63] Loc. cit.

[64] *The Christian Century*, Sept. 3, 1925.

[65] The author's doctoral dissertation, Boston University, 1928, pp. 106, 108f, 113.

[66] See *Civilization and Ethics*, pp. 254f, 263, 264.

[67] Ibid., p. 231.

[68] Ibid., pp. 232, 233, 267.

[69] Ibid., pp. xvi, 251.

[70] Ibid., p. 222.

[71] Loc. cit.

[72] See *Civilization and Ethics*, pp. xiii, xiv, 212f.

[73] Ibid., p. 221f, p. 253.

[74] The author's doctoral dissertation, Boston University, 1928, pp. 234-244.

[75] From Albert Schweitzer, *Memoirs of Childhood and Youth*, p. 44. By permission of The Macmillan Company, publishers.

[76] Ibid., p. 60.

[77] The author's dissertation, Boston University, 1928, pp. 300-303.

[78] See *Civilization and Ethics*.